Why get involved?

What difference can the individual citizen make?

> Sam W. Brown, Jr. believes there is real possibility for change, for building new institutions in our society—through storefront organizing and campaigning.

Here he tells, step by step, how to set up your own storefront organization and how to run it. He tells what happens behind the scenes in a political campaign and the various roles your storefront can play—

> information center, canvassing center, listening post for central headquarters, service center for community projects, and a location for rallies, block parties, and dinners....

He also gives valuable tips on how to get out of the tough spots—

> how to get those all-important phones installed in no time flat, how to deal with managers who won't stuff envelopes and others who only care to be speechwriters, how to avoid high-priced mistakes....

Whatever your cause, whoever your candidate, a veteran organizer and professional campaigner tells how to get results in this hopeful, practical, and complete guidebook to storefront organization and campaigning.

1

STOREFRONT ORGANIZING:

A Mornin' Glories' Manual

SAM W. BROWN, JR.

▲ PYRAMID BOOKS ● NEW YORK

STOREFRONT ORGANIZING

A PYRAMID BOOK

First printing, October 1972

Copyright © 1972 by Sam W. Brown, Jr.

All Rights Reserved

ISBN 0-515-02818-5

Printed in the United States of America

Pyramid Books are published by Pyramid Communications, Inc.
Its trademarks, consisting of the word "Pyramid" and the portrayal
of a pyramid, are registered in the United States Patent Office.

Pyramid Communications, Inc., 919 Third Avenue, New York, N. Y. 10022

To Jesse Unruh who taught me the importance of organization; Eugene McCarthy who showed me that there are some things worth organizing for; and Marty and Anne who remind me that there is much more to life than organizing

TABLE OF CONTENTS

INTRODUCTION

"I can't tell just how many of these movements I've seen started in New York during my forty years in politics, but I can tell you how many have lasted more than a few years —none. There have been reform committees of fifty, of sixty, of seventy, of one hundred and all sorts of numbers that started out to do up the regular political organizations. They were like mornin' glories—looked lovely in the mornin' and withered up in a short time, while the regular machines went on flourishin' forever, like fine old oaks. Say, that's the first poetry I ever worked off. Ain't it great?"

GEORGE WASHINGTON PLUNKETT
City Hall Shoeshine Stand (1890)

This manual is written to help and encourage people who want to organize, but don't know how to start. Whether it's the organization of a political campaign or an issue movement, the basics are the same and I've tried to lay them out here. I've attempted to convey some skills that are indispensable to successful organization.

As a manual it is not definitive and doesn't pretend to be. It can't be complete, and never will be, because finally imagination and inventiveness are the prime ingredients of organizing. If you try something suggested in this book and it works, pass it on; if it doesn't, pass it back to me. Everything here has been tried, and has worked in organizations in which I've had a part; they may not work for you, and I'd like to know that.

Most campaign or organizing manuals pretend to give strategic advice and, in my judgment, all of them fall flat. Strategy is like imagination— the two are closely related. There is no way to teach it—it has to be learned. That means experiencing it, trying it, thinking it over seriously, always being willing to take a step back from the immediate organizational detail and look at the implications of what you're doing. If it becomes clear that the strategy you're pursuing doesn't work, you must be willing to redefine it even though it may require a great deal more work. If you believe in what you're doing, the extra effort is well worth it.

The established political and economic forces always make that extra effort. G. W. Plunkett is one of the most famous of the Tammany organization leaders. His disdain for those who would effect reform, who he refers to as "mornin' glories," is used as a reminder that those who would organize to make change are frequently criticized, berated and consciously obstructed. At the same time, his caustic remarks emphasize the unhappy fact that the attitudes in "politics" and of "politicians" haven't changed much over the years. "It makes my heart bleed to think of it."

I have written this manual in such a manner that it would be usable regardless of ideological persuasion. However, I believe that its real impact will be quite different. The neutrality of this manual is loaded in the same way that the supposed neutrality of a university is loaded. In this case, the bias is against the status quo, rather than for it.

Organization is not magic; it doesn't transform people. It simply makes effective feelings that are present but have never had a chance to direct power. The *few* have always been well organized, the *many* have never been organized and have never had a voice. Grassroots organization is the one way to change that.

Without organization, the best ideas in the world haven't got a chance. The right wing has shown clearly that you don't need to have a new idea in centuries if you have the money and the organization to keep old ideas in power. The left, by definition, will never have the money, but even with limited money, good organization can begin to attack centers of irresponsible power and wealth in America.

Another lesson that should be learned from the right is that even the best organized and best financed effort with no ideas is terribly destructive.

So while this manual tends to be non-ideological it is, I hope, a tool primarily useful to citizen groups who are organizing against the already powerful. And because of its lack of political content it is potentially like all other skills that can

11

be abused and used against the interests of the people rather than on their behalf. To learn to organize without knowing why is as irresponsible as having ideas and not organizing to put them in power.

Finally, organizing, like any other approach to power, can be so diverting as to make us forget to spend time with our friends, forget about the needs of other people—forget to care. When we've forgotten those things, we've lost the reason for trying to organize: we may as well cash it in.

I take full responsibility for any parts of this manual which you may come to regard as wrong-headed or impractical. However, those parts which work well for you and which you regard as helpful are, as with most good things, the result of people working together effectively.

Ted Johnson, now with Senator Gravell's staff, wrote a press manual for the Moratorium which became the foundation for Chapter III.

Mary Meehan wrote a manual on canvassing and election day for the New Democratic Coalition and both Mary and the N.D.C. have graciously permitted me to use it as the basis for Chapter V.

"Storefront Organizing," Chapter I, was first written by me for N.D.C. in 1970, and it has encouraged its use in this manual.

Alison Teal, who managed speakers bureaus for both John Lindsay and Richard Ottinger, gave me invaluable guidance in preparing the material on speakers bureaus.

Lee Sigal, currently at the Brookings Institution, brought George Washington Plunkett to my attention and suggested the sub-title for this manual.

David Mixner, a valued friend and the best

political organizer I know, read much of this manual in manuscript and suggested important changes.

While these friends and others too numerous to mention helped directly, the chain of circumstances which taught me what I know about organizing includes hundreds of people who helped along the way. It is to these people that I am most indebted since they are the ones who finally make everything work in politics as in all other occupations.

Although I am deeply appreciative of the help I've received from all those named and unnamed people, one person more than any other is responsible for the completion of this manual. In the midst of doing other things, Meg Lundstrom always called me back to the task; worked with me on it; had faith in the book; and insisted it could be helpful to others.

I hope she is right.

1

STOREFRONT ORGANIZING

"Have you ever thought what would become of the country if the bosses were put out of business, and their places were taken by a lot of cart-tail orators and college gradua-ates? It would mean chaos. It would be just like takin' a lot of dry-goods clerks and set-tin' them to run express trains on the New York Central Railroad. It makes my heart bleed to think of it. Ignorant people are always talkin' against party bosses, but just wait till the bosses are gone! Then, and not until then, will they get the right sort of epitaphs, as Patrick Henry or Robert Em-met said."

GEORGE WASHINGTON PLUNKETT

What would happen to the country if the bosses were put out of business? And how do you put them out of business?

Every year thousands of people think about it, but only a handful ever attempt to do anything. Unfortunately, the product of most of these attempts is failure. Many of the best ideas and people are lost because of a lack of simple technical organizational skills.

This manual is designed to help more people be more successful in their organizational goals.

The first order of business must be to find a storefront location; staff it with volunteers; and get the mechanism functioning.

FINDING A STOREFRONT LOCATION

When deciding where to have headquarters, place first priority on areas that have the greatest concentration of voters likely to be sympathetic to your candidate, or people interested in your cause. (In general elections always remember that in some areas your candidate may be strong in the primary election, but weak in the general election. Or vice versa.)

Obviously, your local supporters are tremendously important in finding a storefront. Frequently, you can find a real estate agent who will locate property for you rather quickly and who may be willing to find a way to get a reduction in the rent.

In picking the final location, it's probably best not to think in terms of political subdivisions such as district, ward or precinct, or ethnic breakdowns, but rather in terms of the way people function (i.e., shopping centers, media areas, etc.)

If possible, the headquarters should be in the

major shopping area on the main street and ideally on the first floor. Even in concentrated urban areas it's worth the extra expenditure to have a storefront with visibility, as opposed to an office located inside a building. The additional cost usually pays for itself, particularly if you sell a lot of paraphernal a rom the office such as buttons and posters (which can at times be a very successful way to raise money).

If you're in a city large enough for three or four storefronts, you can talk seriously about neighborhood locations. However, if you have only one storefront, it should be in the main shopping area, which is usually the focus of community activity.

Look for good lighting and a large parking area when choosing your headquarters location.

The further you stray from these basic criteria, the less visibility and effectiveness you will have. It's like anything else that you need to convince people about (or sell people on, which is the more crass way of putting it)—you want to be in a place where people have an opportunity both to see you and to see what you're doing.

If you're considering an older building, check the place to make sure there is adequate wiring. There's nothing more embarrassing than getting a place where you can't plug in a mimeograph machine because it will blow out wiring or burn down the building.

Be sure to have some room for privacy. Finding a place with privacy is not necessarily a way of creating a politics of secrecy. It can be simply an area where it's possible to make telephone calls, write letters and hear yourself think. Sometimes this is not easy; you many have to find a way to soundproof part of the headquarters (for example, if you have only one large room).

You will probably have to prevail upon local supporters to guarantee phone, light, heat, and rent. You should prepare them for that when you first talk to them. People shouldn't be startled when they're asked to guarantee $200 of a rent bill, but they almost invariably are. As a consequence, it may be necessary to start fundraising early so you can guarantee those things yourself *before* you open the storefront. Virtually every place will require a rent guarantee, usually for a month.

APPEARANCE

The greatest asset you have in recruiting people in the community is the visibility of your storefront. It should not look the way most peace headquarters look (including the ones that I've worked in). I don't say that in a derogatory way. It's simply that most peace headquarters end up looking like places that most people wouldn't want to come into. They scare people away rather than attract them.

A headquarters must be professional in its appearance. If you're not interested in running a professional-appearing headquarters, you may as well not be there, because you're probably going to offend more people in the community than you win over. The place should be clean and orderly when people come in because most people want to feel comfortable when they visit a headquarters. And they don't feel comfortable if it's messy, or if the walls and floors are dirty.

Be sure to have a large, colorful and attractive sign on the outside of your storefront, with your candidate's name or your cause in huge letters so that anyone driving or walking by can easily identify it. Volunteers from a college or high school art department can probably paint the sign for you. The outside sign is not a luxury—it's an absolute necessity.

Pay special attention to the front section of your headquarters. (You may want to have a partition between the front and back sections, if a great deal of office work is done in the back.) Be sure to have plenty of room for display of literature, buttons, and bumperstrips. It's best to use a literature rack or tables where visitors can just walk along and pick up whatever interests them.

Remember to place a contributions box in the literature section. You might also put a guest book there, if you're trying to develop a good mailing list.

To decorate the windows and walls of your storefront, you can use posters of your candidate and of various causes he's supporting (i.e., peace, ecology, etc.). You might also encourage your art student volunteers to paint some original posters for this purpose.

Avoid the temptation to tape news clippings and cartoons all over the walls. This is one of the quickest ways to make your storefront seem dirty, messy, and cluttered. Put up a bulletin board for the clips and cartoons; don't ruin the walls.

FURNISHING THE STOREFRONT

Your headquarters needn't be plush, by any means. You don't need swivel chairs in order to make the place look decent. It is important, however, what kind of supplies you have and how well they operate to help make the office function smoothly. If done with foresight and planning, office supplies needn't cost a tremendous amount of money. Considerable funds can be saved in equipping the storefront if you use good sense and are resourceful.

Probably the single most expensive item in the office is the telephone. Of course, the actual operating cost depends on how telephones are used and how large an area the storefront is servicing.

A couple of general rules have been helpful to me in the past. One is never to take an answer from the first person you speak with at the telephone company as the final answer. NEVER. Unless that particular person happens to be the President and even then the answer can be misleading.

Almost invariably when you first come into a town, the phone company tells you it will take a minimum of two weeks to get your telephones installed, or ten days, or one week — but never immediately. Don't believe it. You *can* get telephones installed in forty-eight hours. However, to do so you must find somebody important enough in the community to call the appropriate official at the phone company and present your case. Many of us can't make those calls in most towns—but we can usually find someone who can.

The most spectacular instance I was involved with was in Wisconsin. The phone company told us it would take thirty days to get a switchboard installed in our headquarters. This just didn't make any sense at all. We went a little higher in the company and were told they might be able to install it in two or three weeks. Then we called a major financial supporter of the campaign, who in turn called the president of American Telephone and Telegraph Company. That was at four o'clock in the afternoon. At six-thirty the telephone trucks arrived. Two days later, after 48 hours of straight work, we had our telephones.

Few can call the president of A.T.&T., but the local telephone company, through a combination of cajolery and chicanery, can be manipulated into cooperating on a speedy installation. And I *would* exert pressure on them because the first two weeks are going to be tremendously important in terms of soliciting other things in the community and gaining visibility. If people call information, and there's no listing for "Plunkett For President" even though people know there's an office, it can be very embarrassing and can inflict real damage to your cause.

The same tactics apply to the exorbitant deposit requirements—often as high as $500-a-line. Employ the help of influential supporters in the community to avoid these extraordinarily heavy drains on your funds.

The other side of the coin is that once you get the telephones in, they may be a great financial drain on the campaign. It's very easy for everybody to pick up the telephone and call friends, neighbors, relatives, college friends, the button manufacturer on Long Island, or anybody it occurs to them to call, and it's very hard to control the misuse of the phone.

If you ask the phone company, they will put an interruption operator on the telephone line so that whenever somebody direct-dials a long-distance number, an operator comes on and says, "May I have your number, please?" If you ask for it, the phone company will issue you a billing code, which is usually an eight- or nine-digit number. Otherwise, if anybody simply gives your telephone number, the operator will put through the call. However, if you tell everybody in the office that they must have a billing code and put a sign on the phone that says "Billing Code required on all long-distance calls," it's possible to discourage almost everyone from making unnecessary long-distance calls.

If you have real problems with misuse of your telephones, you can simply put locks on some of them or have only "in" lines on some of them.

One way to control the long-distance call problem is by the use of a WATS line, which stands for Wide Area Telephone Service. WATS lines are available on either a timed or unlimited time basis. In the first instance, you pay for ten hours of actual time use (that is, if you call someone and talk for twenty-three seconds, you're billed for twenty-three seconds) and additional time beyond the first ten hours is sold at a certain cost per hour. On an unlimited time schedule, you make all the calls you want and are billed a single, but much higher fee. With this arrangement you should be prepared to use that phone almost constantly, establishing some type of system to insure its constant use.

WATS lines can also be divided another way— state-wide or zone. Zoning is controlled by concentric circles from the phone's origin, with an additional cost for each added zone. The radius of each circle is about two hundred miles.

The costs for WATS lines can be extraordinary, but in the final analysis, if you need ten hours a month or more of long-distance phone time, WATS lines are good investments.

Be careful of one thing. Because of the great dependence on telephones in political campaigns, a strange psychology has developed whereby many campaigners regard letters as less important than phone calls. This is a great mistake. You never know when a simple request for information on the candidate's or organization's views may come from a voter who will vote for your candidate if his letter is answered promptly; or from a person who may contribute money; or from a national group that may offer technical aid or endorse your candidate or cause. Answer all letters promptly and well, and don't lean too heavily on the telephone.

Be sure to have a large bulletin board for phone messages in your headquarters. Print in large letters on the board the name of each staff member or full-time volunteer, and see that all phone messages are promptly tacked beneath the appropriate name. Another method often used is to have a wall-hanging shoebag with the name of each staff member on each of the pockets; all phone messages and mail can be immediately placed in the appropriate pocket.

Of course, office furniture is necessary, and if you quickly establish contacts in the community, most of your volunteer room can be furnished for free. It is possible to get your standard eight-foot church basement table with matching folding chairs on loan from a friendly church. You can obtain the use of other supplies at no cost simply by asking people to bring in old but usable ball-point pens and other office supplies from their office or home.

My own feeling is that for the small expenditures, particularly paper, pens, pencils, erasers, staplers, rubber bands, and paper clips, the marginal difference in cost of buying them (a total cost of perhaps $20 for all those supplies) as opposed to depending on hand-me-downs is so small as to not justify wasting time scrounging for them. However, if you have more time than money, it's possible to save a little bit here.

Most operations in which I've been involved have never had enough money to purchase desks outright at the beginning, which is a shame because you end up paying more for them over a period of time. If you stay in business six or eight months, you pay in rental costs the price of the same furniture, and at the end, of course, you have nothing left. But such is the high cost of being poor, and in most cities, the rental of desks and other basic office furnishings can be quite easily arranged.

To produce your own literature of the highest quality at the lowest cost, I have found that Gestetner products are clearly superior to others that may be available in terms of quality of print, flexibility of use, cost and speed of repair, and speed and dependability of production (i.e., the machine rarely picks up five or six sheets of paper and then prints one). In addition, they have a system which includes a wonderful machine called the Gestifax, which is an electric stencil producer which will reproduce quite easily any printed page or graphic you might want to use The machine is tremendously expensive, about $2000 However, in most communities where there is a Gestetner dealer, they will make electric stencils for you for about $2.50 each. These stencils are good for 8,000 to 10,000 impressions. In that way you can reproduce materials, including such things as bar graphs, without the tedious task of scratching them by hand onto stencils.

However, it makes no sense to buy paper from Gestetner, for any of the cheaper papers will give equally good impressions. In addition, Gestetner paper tends to flake off onto the stencil which then needs cleaning more frequently in order to maintain a good impression without little black dots all over it.

Photocopiers become almost as indispensable as they are in any kind of modern office. Some of the lesser known models are substantially less expensive than Xerox. However, if quality of reproduction is important to you and you intend to use it for a large number of copies, Xerox is by far the superior machine. The additional costs may well prove worth it if the end product is more effective and efficiently produced.

You can almost always get a twenty to twenty-five percent discount on office supplies by buying them through the same outlet all the time; by "placing an order" rather than buying single items, one at a time; and, by having your order delivered.

It is a good idea to have stationery printed on low-cost paper which you can use for mass mailings; for mimeographing letters and press releases (if you don't have special press stationery) and for other high-quantity operations. In addition, you should have some high-quality, twenty-five percent rag content stationery printed for use in fund-raising letters, letters seeking support from office-holders, executives, union officials, and community leaders, simply because it makes a good impression. It makes no sense to print stationery in black since it costs no more to print it in another color which gives you a pleasing contrast for typed letters.

It's possible to avoid printing envelopes by stamping the return address with a rubber stamp. If you have a large number of volunteers and a lot of time, that may make sense. My feeling is that, unless you want to appear super-poor, the cost differential to have envelopes printed is very small, and that the expense is justified by the impression made upon the people receiving them.

You might try to get a graphic artist to donate his design services for a pleasant stationery layout. However, multi-color printing and photographs on stationery are, I feel, an unnecessary additional expenditure.

OPENING THE HEADQUARTERS

It's a good idea to have a "grand opening" for your storefront. Try to arrange to have your candidate or a well-known representative there to cut the ribbon (if that ceremony doesn't seem too old-fashioned for your area) and to circulate and chat with the community people. Have refreshments on hand and a pleasant, party atmosphere. Be sure to invite the press, since a headquarters opening is always a good occasion for publicity.

Be sure your candidate and prominent local supporters stop by the storefront and chat with people whenever they are in the area. This is a great morale boost for your staff and volunteers. And if your candidate also does a bit of street campaigning in the area, word will get around that he's interested in the community and its problems.

Your storefront should be open from nine A.M. to nine P.M. at least. Some people feel that a storefront should be open even longer. They believe that staff should be willing to work an eighteen- or twenty-hour day throughout the campaign. I was once of that school, but was wrong. Effectiveness decreases as weariness increases, and if you get a decent amount of rest, you'll be more efficient in your work and less likely to snap and growl at other staff, volunteers, and storefront visitors.

FRIENDLINESS

When people come in, they should feel that they're wanted. They shouldn't have to wander around, picking up literature and idly looking at things and then finally having to say, "Hey, what's happening here?" before somebody comes up and politely says, "Hi! Is there something we can do? Would you like to see more literature? Would you like to help us out?" People feel more comfortable when you can offer them a cup of coffee and say you'd like to talk to them about the campaign or the cause.

In most local headquarters, recruiting twenty volunteers is probably the most important thing you can do in the first week or ten days. Twenty reliable volunteers permit you to set up a work schedule which doesn't demand twenty-two hours a day of your time. They will permit you to have local people and local voices on the telephone and visibility from older people in the storefront all the time.

Take time to make people feel important when they come in your storefront. If you can offer them that cup of coffee, a friendly hand, and some conversation, they'll more than likely come back again. If they don't plan to come back, they'll probably be embarrassed enough to pay 50¢ for a button—and that's 50¢ you didn't have before.

You should have someone who answers the telephone in a mature voice and in the dialect of the local community. In New Hampshire we hired a lady to answer the telephone simply because she said "McCa'ty for President"—and none of the rest of us could ever say "McCa'ty" quite the way it's said in New Hampshire. She sat at the desk and answered the telephone all day long. She didn't know anything about politics; but she answered the telephone effectively. Finding such a person is a very good expenditure of time and energy.

Don't let telephone calls be lost, and don't let callers wait forever. Don't shout at other people around the room when people are talking on the telephone and avoid interrupting anyone who is talking on the phone. You can't afford to let rudeness be the impression you give to the community.

COMMUNITY SUPPORT

There are several places to begin finding support in the community, support which will provide a continuing base of volunteers and local knowledge.

The membership lists of potentially friendly organizations are important. Some of these turn out to be obvious, and some obscure. American Civil Liberties Union attorneys and members of the American Association of University Professors are frequently helpful, as may be members of the American Association of University Women and the American Association for the United Nations. It's also sometimes possible to get mailing lists from the American Friends Service Committee, Americans for Democratic Action, Business Executives Move for Vietnam Peace, local service clubs, such as the American Association of University Women, and the League of Women Voters, the Vietnam Vets Against the War, the list of precinct workers for a political party, and other similar organizations.

You should also seek out people who were active in the Moratorium, in the 1968 McCarthy and Kennedy campaigns, or in other efforts similar to what you are planning.

Check church groups in the area. The Unitarians, the Congregationalists, and the local rabbi are frequently the most sympathetic for liberal candidates and causes; the Baptists and the Assembly of God members for conservatives.

If you're working in an area outside your home community, you must get local people deeply involved in the campaign or organization in a public and visible way. You should not be the person who opens a storefront, has a press conference, talks to the press. You should find ways to make yourself secondary to the local personalities. It's very difficult to do that at times, especially when the press comes walking in the door and wants to talk to whoever is in charge. It's not easy to say, "Well, gee, he's not in right now. Why don't you go down the street and find him at his business?" —when you know that in fact the person is rarely in and probably isn't going to be available. Yet it's tremendously important that visibility be from a local standpoint.

If you are in a university community, you should try to recruit students, for they often are one of the prime sources of local energy and enthusiasm. The editors of campus newspapers can be very helpful in motivating and influencing the student community. There are also the obvious methods of posters, newspaper ads, telephone tree handbills and mobile speakers.

One method that is slightly different but works well is the tent-like card: 3x5 cards are printed on a mimeograph machine and each card is folded in the middle so it makes an open tent shape. The cards are placed on tables all over the student union, the cafeterias, the library, dormitory lounges—anywhere people congregate. If you leave the tent cards on tables, people pick them up, look at them, and set them back down again. They're very effective.

VOLUNTEER RECRUITMENT

Essential to any campaign is a form to recruit volunteers. This can be passed out at meetings, sent in a mailing to potential supporters, and made available on the literature table of your storefront. Following is a suggestion for a 3 x 5 card:

FRONT

NAME_____

ADDRESS_____

OFFICE PHONE_____HOME PHONE_____

I'm available for work on the following days and hours:

	morn.	aft.	even.		morn.	aft.	even.
Mon.	____	____	____	Fri.	____	____	____
Tues.	____	____	____	Sat.	____	____	____
Wed.	____	____	____	Sun.	____	____	____
Thurs.	____	____	____				

BACK

I would like to do the following type(s) of work:

____Art work	____Leafleting
____Bookkeeping	____Literature Dist.
____Canvassing	____Mimeographing
____Clipping	____Photography
____Driving	____Press work
____Fundraising	____Research
____General office work	____Telephoning
	____Typing

If you have a car for errands, check here _____

If you would like to poll watch, check here_____

Of course, the form must be tailored to meet the needs of your campaign. Poll watching may not be important in your area, or it may be the difference between winning and losing.

Be sure that everyone who fills out the form is contacted shortly thereafter and asked to do something specific, or (in the case of those who can work only on election day) thanked for their offer to help and told they will be contacted again later on.

You'll want to keep the forms in a file box for quick reference when help is needed. You might arrange them alphabetically by last name, with a cross index that lists the names under each category of work. You'll find this file enormously helpful in setting up work schedules and in finding extra volunteers for special tasks.

It's useful to have an orientation sheet for volunteers, especially if your office is so large that you cannot supervise everyone individually. You could include on this sheet information on how to answer the phone, where to find office supplies, how to run the machines, "housekeeping tips" on cleaning up, and a list of useful addresses and phone numbers.

You might also consider having a newsletter for your volunteers and other local supporters. This may be a mimeographed sheet that appears twice a month. It should include information on your candidate's schedule, your canvassing plans, your special volunteer needs, when and where supporters can get yard signs, and any other information you want to circulate.

Just be sure to keep a newsletter very practical in its purpose and effect. In any type of political work, there's always a temptation to talk too much to the converted, telling them what they already know, instead of reaching out to those who haven't yet received your message. The converted should be out converting other people, and you should be providing practical information to help them do this.

Of course, if finances permit, you might have a newsletter done with offset printing and used as a regular feature of your literature table or in canvassing. In this case, you would want to combine substantive messages with practical information.

VOLUNTEERS

It's tremendously important to develop jobs which are not vital but which are sufficiently responsible so that volunteers feel involved until you can check them out. The first time somebody comes into the office, you have to have something for them to do. You can't simply say, "Gee, if you can come back tomorrow morning, I'll have something." You should always have a roster of things which have to be done and which people can do—whether they're high school volunteers who walk in the storefront, volunteers who are called in, or volunteers who come in on a regular work schedule. If volunteers don't feel they're being useful, you'll not see them again.

On the other hand, you don't want to give the most important jobs to people until you've had a chance to look at what they can do. Therefore, it's necessary—even with the people who come in and want to be speechwriters (and you'll get a number of those)—to set up work tasks which, if they're really committed, they're going to be willing to do anyway.

In one campaign I was involved in, we were sitting in the basement and addressing envelopes at three o'clock in the morning. The campaign manager came down, and stood there watching us work. One of the people there was a graduate student in Chinese; he said, "You know, in China there's an ancient tradition that at the beginning of the agricultural season, when the time comes to begin the planting, the emperor takes a silver spade and goes out and turns the first shovelful of dirt." At that point the campaign manager sat down and began addressing envelopes.

It's very important that everybody be willing to pitch in no matter what the task. If you're superior to the volunteers, they are not going to do anything you won't do. You'll end up doing the work because the volunteers won't be there to do it. You may as well recognize that at the start and understand that it's important to involve yourself in even the most routine tasks.

You have to demand this of the new volunteers, too. If a guy comes in and wants to be a speechwriter, you say, "Fine. But see that stack of envelopes? We need your handwriting techniques first. We'll get to the speeches later. Let's get the other things done now."

At the same time, you can't keep people addressing envelopes forever. You have to move them on to doing other things. And hopefully all of us will discover some alternative to the Peter Principle, so that at four months the campaign is not an operation in which everyone reaches their level of incompetence, but one in which people are doing jobs they can do well.

You must develop a work schedule which has something for everyone to do, and you have to elevate people as they go along. You can't keep them in drudge work forever if you expect them to keep coming back.

The best workers on most office tasks are housewives. If you can get these women coming into your office, they can be one of the greatest assets you have. Most of them don't like to go out and leaflet; they just don't like to stand on street corners. But they'll do everything in the office—they'll address envelopes all day long.

Try to have someone other than yourself in the office all the time and on a regular basis. Many people will be willing to come in one day a week. You should set up a regular work schedule so you always have someone there (and someone who can do a good deal of the work).

THE STOREFRONT AS COMMUNITY CENTER

If your campaign is well financed, or if you have many organizers who can support storefronts through local fundraising, you may have a large number of storefronts.

However, if your campaign has only one or two headquarters, then those headquarters must concentrate on servicing the entire district. In that case they are likely to be office operations in the traditional sense and are likely to serve the communities in which they're located only in a passive way. If you have *many* headquarters around your district, then just one or two of them need worry about servicing the entire district. Each of the others can concentrate on its own community. Instead of passively providing information upon request, the storefront can reach out into the community and organize it for your candidate.

Viewed in this light, a storefront can be used for many roles:

1. *Information Center.* Draw community residents in to talk about the candidate and the

campaign by the visibility and attractiveness of your storefront. Give them literature, buttons, and bumperstrips. Recruit many of them to help with the campaign.

2. *Canvassing Center.* Use the storefront as the center for all canvassing in the area. Prepare voting lists and precinct maps in the storefront. Train and debrief your canvassers there.

3. *Listening Post for Central Headquarters.* Let your central headquarters know what issues your voters are most concerned about and how they are reacting to your candidate. Collect information for the advance/scheduling team at central headquarters so they'll know how best to plan the candidate's appearances in your area. (They will need information on both the politics and the logistics of your community.)

4. *Service Center.* In one mayoralty campaign, special volunteers were available in the candidate's storefronts to explain a new and complicated city rent law. Many voters had a personal stake in this law, so the service was well received. You might use your storefront as the center for a neighborhood clean-up project. This will dramatize your candidate's concern about the environment and also provide a service to the community.

In devising a service project, keep two rules in mind: one, it must suit the needs of the community; and two, it must suit the background and major concerns of your candidate or cause. If these rules are neglected, the project will seem useless, superficial, and Johnny-come-lately.

5. *Location for Block Parties.* Provide some refreshments and entertainment, and invite everyone in the neighborhood to come. Try to have your candidate or a well-known representative there, not for a formal reception, but just to chat

informally with the neighborhood people. Have all your literature, buttons and bumperstrips on special display. Have staff and volunteers circulate, talk up the campaign, and recruit volunteers in a soft-sell way.

6. *Location for Coffees*. Invite all the voters in the neighborhood to a coffee where they can meet your candidate and discuss the issues with him. Again, use the opportunity to recruit volunteers as well as votes.

INFORMATION YOU MAY NEED

It is possible to develop immense amounts of research. I'll run through some of the things which it may be productive to develop early in the campaign:

1. Names of the political figures in the community, including elected party officials.

2. The composition of the community in terms of ethnic groups and housing patterns.

3. The distribution of the community in terms of blue-collar, white-collar (employment statistics, basically), and a general look at the economy of the area (i.e. local industries, unemployment rates).

4. Voter registration statistics and voting patterns of the last four years. You have to develop a variety of statistics in order to have some prediction of off-year election turnouts. You might check the last mayoralty race, the vote for the Congressman in the congressional primary the last time around, the gubernatorial election, and the presidential election. There is no absolute method you can use to know exactly what the turnout is going to be. It's guesswork, but you should end up

with some idea of the numbers with which you're working.

5. The media in the area, with the telephone numbers and news editors. (This includes radio, TV, and pencil press.)
6. Important business, social, religious, fraternal and ethnic organizations in the area, and a list of groups which may be available for recruiting purposes (student and women's organizations for example).
7. Attitude surveys of the area if there are any available. (Check local universities.)
8. Maps of the community in various kinds of detail (especially for canvassing).
9. The community calendar (list of coming events in the community), usually available through the neighborhood newspaper, the local community center, churches, and schools.
10. Information on the opposition's leadership.
11. A list of shopping centers, parks, gathering places, factories, movies, and office buildings which you'll use later on for literature distribution. (When you get a factory's address and the number of employees, you should also get the time of shift changes, because that is obviously the time it's important to be there.)

Now, having said all of that, there are three or four of those things which you'll find useful. The rest of it, I suspect, is nonsense.

The media file, the community calendar, the list of organizations which you can use, and the list of shopping centers, parks, and other gathering places will probably be very important to you as you move through the campaign. The other things are useful in getting an overview of your community, but they're usually not as helpful in a practical sense.

However, if you have limited energy available, you must make some judgments with regard to where you work first. And for that, it's going to be tremendously important to have some statistical breakdown by precinct.

TIPS ON PRINTING AND MAILING

Hopefully, the central headquarters will have literature which you can use. But you may have to prepare some of your own for local use in leafleting and mailing.

One thing many of us fail to remember is that mimeographing is not as acceptable outside the academic community as it is inside the academic community. Mimeographed things are of marginal utility, since they are usually of poor quality and lack a professional polish.

Having said that, I'll make an exception to it. The exception is the electro-stencil which permits you to use graphics. If any of you have ever attempted graphics on a regular mimeograph stencil, you know they come out looking less than minimally satisfactory. An electro-stencil can take care of that. It can do professional, small-league printing. If run properly, it looks almost as good as offset printing. (Photographs, however, do not come out very well on an electro-stencil.)

You can also make mimeographed material more respectable by the quality of paper and the kind of fold that you use. A mimeographed piece with triple folding into a little brochure can look reasonably presentable.

For internal communications and for communications among the committed, mimeograph is perfectly acceptable. And, of course, for advertising coming events the mimeograph is indispensable.

Be sure to check the weight of your paper when

planning a mailing. One extra sheet of paper may cost you an extra 8¢ per envelope. That may not seem like much, but if you're doing a mailing of 5,000 pieces and you discover when you get down to the post office that it's going to cost an extra $300 because you forgot and put in an extra sheet of paper, you're going to be pretty angry with yourself, not to mention the unnecessary drain on your funds.

If maximum words delivered by mail with minimum delay is important to you, it is possible to print both sides of five sheets of blue sixteen-pound paper; stuff it in number nine envelopes; and with a stamp and label still be under one ounce.

(If you print on twenty-pound paper or use number ten envelopes you will be overweight. If you use any sixteen-pound paper other than blue, you can't print on both sides since the print will bleed through the paper.)

The same is true of basic campaign literature. Before you print a brochure, stick the mock-up into an envelope and weigh it so that if you decide to mass-mail the brochure, you can do it on one stamp.

In New Hampshire we were doing a mailing of 110,000 pieces and discovered that the item was one-sixteenth of an ounce overweight because the printer in New York had used the wrong weight of paper. With a 110,000-piece mailing, it would have cost approximately $7,000 more to mail it. So after having stuffed the whole mailing, we had to unstuff it, take it back to the printer, and run it through a cutter to cut off about an eighth of an inch from the bottom. Then we had to take it back, refold it, and restuff it. In addition to requiring a lot of extra work, it was *very* embarrassing.

There's been some debate over the effectiveness of direct mailing, and its success or failure in your particular campaign depends on your candidate. If he has very little name identification in the area, it's probably helpful for people to receive some direct literature. If, however, there is high name identification and you're attempting to do issue identification, literature mailing probably is of marginal value.

There's another debate on the best class of postage to use. In this chapter I've given figures for first-class mailing for two reasons: one, if you mail first class, you don't have to count, bundle, and tie by zip code area; and two, I assume all of us have a similar attitude toward junk mail—we throw a piece of third-class mail into the waste basket.

The other school of thought says that you should do a piece which has the candidate's name in big letters on the outside, addressed directly on the outside, and is mailed third-class. Even if people never open it, at least they've seen the name one more time.

Another alternative is a literature drop which stuffs your brochure under the door at each residence (house or apartment). It should be much cheaper than mailing, but if you have to bring in volunteers from outside to do the literature drop and house them and feed them you're better off using the mails.

In any event, it's good to have a cover letter which is signed by someone known and respected by the people you're sending it to. If you're mailing to the ACLU (American Civil Liberties Union) list, you may as well have the local president of the ACLU, if he's with you, write and sign a printed cover letter.

Or you might use a cover letter to introduce your storefront. It's a way of introducing yourself and telling people they're welcome to come over.

SPEAKERS BUREAU

A speakers bureau is one very effective way of getting the word out about your candidate or cause. Many organizations, from Rotary Clubs to PTAs, are begging for speakers. Fulfill that need, and your presence in the community will be felt.

Organizing a speakers bureau is basically a matter of soliciting the speakers, soliciting the engagements, and then putting the two together.

You'll probably have two types of speakers— high priority, those persons with a recognized name in the community, and those not well known who are nonetheless able speakers. Use the first for special engagements; use the second as much as you can.

You can solicit speakers through recommendations of the candidate or persons already involved in the organization; through mailings to special groups of your supporters such as lawyers, teachers and clergymen; and as part of a mass mailing sent to your constituency.

Sometimes you'll have the person's reputation as a speaker to go on; othertimes you'll just have to send him or her out and hope for the best. Check back with the organization on reaction to the speaker, and keep a record of it.

After you have speakers and before you send them out, hold an orientation program at a con-convenient time, explaining your organization's goals, structure, policy stands or your candidate's view on major issues. This session should be short and intense, and should leave all the speakers with a feeling they can handle any situation they encounter. It is helpful to prepare briefing sheets or speakers manuals presenting the main issues and summarizing the important arguments they may have to use.

Keep a file on each speaker, with the times he is available and the engagements he has handled recorded on it. If you like, on the back record relevant comments on his ability.

Solicit the speaking engagements by sending out a letter to each and every organization you can: environmental, political, educational, civic, and religious. You can find a list of these organizations in the phone book, and some libraries and community agencies have more complete lists.

The letter should say you have speakers available for club programs, and should include a postcard they can mail back to you. The card should provide space for them to describe their organization and give figures on estimated attendance at the program for which they want you. (This last item is important — it's a great mistake to send a high-powered speaker to a meeting where five people show.)

Once you have the organization's request, match it up with a speaker who seems appropriate for the group. Notify the speaker by phone to see if he or she can handle the engagement, and then send a letter as another reminder. Two or three days before the speech, call the speaker again. Few things are more embarrassing—and harder to explain — than a missed speaking engagement.

2

FUNDRAISING

"The civil service gang is always howlin'
about candidates and officeholders puttin'
up money for campaigns and about corpora-
tions chippin' in. They might as well howl
about contributions to churches. A political
organization has to have money for its business as well as a church, and who has more
right to put up than the men who get the
good things that are goin'?"

GEORGE WASHINGTON PLUNKETT

It is easy to ask people to donate their time and their efforts, to loan a car or to contribute a bed for a volunteer and get positive results. It's very difficult to ask for cash and get the same tangible results. It's as if money was more valuable than, and somehow different from, time and energy.

Yet if people are sympathetic, asking for money should be no different than asking for time.

Not everyone finds it difficult to ask for money. Aimee Semple McPherson, who ran the Four Square Gospel Tabernacle in Southern California, was known to string clotheslines down the aisles in front of parishioners with clothespins on them. She then called upon people to pin their contributions—folding money only—to the clothesline so that other people could see what they had given. Most of us find the asking much more painful.

In raising funds, campaigns and organizations often face a classic "chicken-egg" situation—it's impossible to attract people's attention without starter money, and it's impossible to get starter money without first attracting attention. The simple solution is to appeal to a few large donors in the absence of a broad base of support. The alternative is to do the outlandish, thus attracting attention without spending money. Since the second method raises more problems than money, the first is almost always used. This, however, raises a major difficulty of fundraising—it often creates a sense of responsibility to large donors. When a large donor calls on the phone, he usually makes his presence known in the smallest or largest organization—frequently a much heavier presence than a person who gives a greater equivalent of time and energy to a campaign. It's not fair, but it's common human reaction, for we all become, in some way or another, dependent on money.

As soon as possible, you *must* create a broad base of support to avoid the very clear danger of single-source funding. John Gardner, the founder of Common Cause, started that organization with substantial donations from five men. At a rally in Denver later that year, someone challenged his idea of citizen funding and control of the organization, pointing to the large initial contributors. Gardner responded by saying, "It's not where your money came from in the past that's important to an organization—it's where it's going to come from in the future." (Gardner did, in fact, pay back the five contributors with money from the $15 membership fees of Common Cause members.) If you take definite steps to insure that future funding is from a large number of small donors, you will find your resistance to demands of past large donors much stronger.

In listing methods of fundraising, let's start with those which are most broad-based even though they may not be possible from the very beginning, and work from there to those methods which are less desirable in some ultimate sense but which may be the easiest ways to raise the original money.

There is one cardinal rule of fundraising: no source of funding is so small that you can afford to ignore it.

PARAPHERNALIA SALES

One of the best examples of broad-based fundraising from small contributors was the Mailer-Breslin mayoralty campaign in New York in 1969. While Norman Mailer himself was putting up substantial sums of money, the campaign nonetheless raised thousands of dollars through sales of paraphernalia on the streets—buttons, bumper-strips, and other forms of small solicitation.

One important element is mandatory for success in early sales of this type—the candidate or the cause must be well-known enough so that people will pay to exhibit their support. This can be done in one of two ways, if your candidate or cause does not already have a wide reputation or following: first, you can focus the initial thrust of your campaign on a specific audience which is easily accessible, such as a college campus, and expand from there, through small contributions, into the larger community; or you can make an easily identifiable issue the focus of the campaign (such as peace or ecology) and use its symbol in buttons and posters.

Buttons and bumperstrips can be produced easily and quickly and then sold on street corners, at shopping centers, headquarters, fundraising parties, and in some cases, such as environmental campaigns, through sympathetic stores like headshops and bookstores. Buttons can be produced in small or large quantities. Two color (light background and single printed color) celluloid buttons can be produced for about $55 or $65 per thousand in $1\frac{1}{4}$ or $1\frac{1}{2}$ inch size. In larger quantities, metal litho buttons are definitely cheaper. They can be purchased in the same size and color for around $30 per thousand in quantities of 10,-000 and for under $20 per thousand in quantities of 50,000 or more.

You can either do your own design or have the button company design the button for you. The main criteria for buttons is to keep the colors bright with high-contrast and to keep the wording to a minimum. It is a good idea to create a symbol for your campaign which is easily identifiable and which can be printed on the buttons with few or no words with it. In the case of a campaign where a candidate's name is needed, simply the name and a small symbol on a distinctive button is effective. "In-group" buttons, such as the small ½ inch "Eugene" button or the FMBNH (For McCarthy Before New Hampshire) buttons of 1968 will not sell in large quantities, although they can be sold at higher prices at fundraising and morale-building parties. Buttons can be sold on the street for 25¢ to 50¢ each. They sell best at senior citizen centers and on high school and college campuses.

Bumperstrips are an effective way, in most cities, to raise substantial amounts of money in small quantities. The same rules of design apply as with buttons—the name of the candidate or a very simple one or two word slogan should be evident in high contrast, relatively dark colors.

Prices of bumperstrips vary widely depending on the size, quality and type of paper used. Experience has shown that it's best to use better quality bumperstrips for two reasons: one, they won't fade in strong light and bad weather and, if there's any substantial period of time involved, they wear well and remain identifiable; secondly, when the time comes they are easier to remove. The cheaper the bumperstrip, the stickier and messier it is to take off—it tends to shred rather than come off in just a few pieces.

Posters are an easy way to raise money. In a campaign involving environmental or peace issues, you can often find local artists with the talent to design posters which can then be sold for several dollars each. Printing costs will usually run around 20¢-30¢ each, depending on the number of colors and size of the poster. They are a great profit-making item, and if especially well done, their sales may soar even if your campaign stands still.

MAILINGS

A second, relatively impersonal form of broad-based fundraising is through the use of mailings. Success depends upon three things: first, the potential excitement of the cause or candidate; second, the mood and feeling of the time; third, the quality of the mailing.

In general, two kinds of lists are used. One is that of friends, acquaintances, and political mailing lists developed from past campaigns or efforts. A second general kind of mailing list is that of magazines, local newspapers, and so forth. Frequently national magazines make mailing lists available at a cost of approximately $30-$40 per thousand names. Local specialty newspapers with subscriber lists, such as ethnic papers, environmental papers, and journalism reviews will occasionally make mailing lists available to causes with which they are sympathetic, but they rarely sell their lists. You can obtain them through personal contact and discussion.

The percentage of returns from direct mail solicitations is very difficult to gauge, but a return of three or four percent is usually regarded as good. There have been so many fundraising mailings recently to most of the available national lists that there is a possibility of diminishing return. Occasionally, however, on a particularly sexy project or through the mailing list you've personally developed, returns of a higher percentage are possible.

It is probably easier to raise money from magazine lists in a non-election year since there are so many demands upon these people during an election year. Names from magazines and political lists are of people who are already politically aware and who have certainly received other mailings. On the other hand, the political consciousness of the general population is higher during election years, and if you can find ways to reach them through direct mail channels, they will probably contribute more than in off years.

Professional associations will sometimes make their mailing lists available. It is frequently worthwhile to send mailings to names taken from the yellow pages of local phone directories, such as attorneys and doctors, where there is a tie-in with their professional interests and the issue at hand.

Another source of potential contributors is the entire faculty list or a department list from the back of a college catalog. Church lists of potentially sympathetic people may also be helpful. For instance, a list of Unitarians may be helpful to liberal candidates, and letters to members of Southern Baptist churches may help conservative candidates.

Organizations while formed around another issue, whose membership may be sympathetic to yours are often a good source of mailing lists. For instance, for environmental action, a mailing sent to members of the American Friends Service Committee might be productive. In most instances, these mailing lists will not be for sale. Sometimes, however, a trade may be desired, although obviously you will have to exercise discretion in deciding with whom you should trade. When people contribute to a specific cause, they don't want to be solicited by everyone else as a result of that one donation. So if you plan to build a long-term organization, it is better not to make your mailing list available to more than a very, very limited number of people. Even then, it should be given only under very special circumstances and for one time, never multiple, use.

If you want to gauge the effectiveness of different mailing lists, you can code the envelopes or return coupons by strategically locating a small symbol, or varying the text slightly. If you have a number of mailing lists but can only afford to use a few of them, you can code a sample mailing of fifty people on each list, and then from the results decide which list to mail *in toto*.

Second-party solicitation is another possibility —that is, to have someone who is already a contributor and is well known write to others on your behalf. Although obviously a much superior method of solicitation, it is difficult because it requires that people spend their political chits with political friends and impose upon their personal friends. However, if you can get people to do it, it's a very effective way to raise money.

A slight variation on this is to get professionals, such as prominent lawyers and professors, to sign letters to others of their profession on your behalf. Use extreme caution here because frequently the person most friendly to you and your cause may very well not be highly regarded by many of his colleagues in the community. Find out what kind of general reactions people have to an individual (a sensitive business) before sending letters over that person's signature.

The best way to insure that a second-party letter is actually sent is to write the letter yourself and have the signatory approve it. Then you type it, prepare the envelopes, have the signatory sign it, and mail it yourself. This assures that the letter is done the way you want it done and gets out on time. If you leave everything up to the signatory, it frequently doesn't get done.

Because of the plethora of direct mail fundraising campaigns on all sides of the political spectrum, the most effective letter is a direct, straightforward, short appeal for funds. Don't burden people with a great deal of material which they probably won't read anyway.

All fundraising mailings should have a professional appearance. There's no point in sending out mimeographed or poorly-printed fundraising material. The additional expenditure for a professional job more than pays for itself in added contributions. (Even those people who don't contribute should be left with a feeling that they were asked to be part of a competent organization.) By the same token, however, two-color mailings on high-quality stationery are wasted money.

For larger contributors, however, personal-appearing letters from the candidate, the campaign manager, or the organizer of the effort on high quality paper, individually typed or robo-typed and mailed in personal-sized envelopes are a good investment. A robotype can usually be rented. An operator (who can be easily trained) punches a master tape, then inserts a single sheet of stationery into the machine, types the inside address and the salutation, punches a button, and the body of the letter is automatically typed. Robotyped letters give the complete impression of an individually-typed letter by producing through actual keypunching the look and feel of typing.

If your effort is large enough to justify the use of computer lists and labeling, it is possible to have letters produced with the name of the addressee in the salutation and twice in the body of the letter, including a simulated signature. Computer letters are printed by heat transfer methods, which have the look, though not the feel, of actual typing. The insertion of the name of the addressee in the body of the letter gives the impression of a personal letter. It requires, however, the considerable investment of the computer programming and keypunching of the addressee, in addition to the expense of running each letter. While this is a high price to pay for a random list, it may be functional in the second go-around for known contributors.

One convenient way to make address labels is to type them on 8½ x 11 sheets of labels, 33 labels to a page, which you can find in any stationery store. Xerox manufactures a pre-gummed paper for Xerox machine use, and by using your typed list, you can copy addresses in a clean, easy, ready-to-use fashion. You can then use one copy of your list for an alphabetical file, another copy for a reverse file by addresses, other copies for mailings, and so on.

Postage-paid return envelopes are a very good investment. Use a no. 6¾ return envelope with a large closure flap that permits people to give personal information (name, address, telephone) which you can tear off and file, or include a 3x5 card for this information. Either of these two items inserted in a #9 or #10 envelope with two sheets of paper will still be safely under the one-ounce limit requiring an 8¢ stamp. Since no fund-raising letter should be longer than two pages, this works out quite well.

For every contribution that comes in, you must send a thank-you note. Even if the donation is only $1, the contributor deserves the courtesy of knowing that you've received the money and that you're appreciative. A thank-you post card is adequate for small contributions. Here is a good example:

> this, as citizens, we all inherit.
> this is ours, to love and live upon,
> and use wisely down all the
> generations of the future.
>
> This is The American Earth.
>
> thank you for your contribution.
> Citizens for Colorado's future

Personally-typed (or robotyped) thank-you letters should be sent for every contribution above a certain point (usually $25 or $50), and contributions of $100 and more deserve a very personal thank-you note from the candidate or director of the campaign if possible.

RALLIES

Passing the hat and selling buttons and posters at rallies is a good way to raise money. The biggest fund raising mistake in the world is to forget the rally. The New York Moratorium made almost $70,000 through sales and donations at a single rally.

If you get a hundred or two hundred people listening to a congressional candidate, you ought to be able to come up with 50¢ a head. Sell buttons; sell posters; pass buckets; implore them from the speaker's stand. In every possible way, ask people for money. It's a tragic mistake to forget that, because it's pure profit. It costs nothing, and you can make a lot of money from it.

Be sure to check for possible legal restrictions on public fund solicitation before making the pitch at rallies.

PARTIES

A very traditional way of raising money is through having parties. The all-time standard party is, of course, the cocktail party, of which there are three general types: high admission, low admission, and no admission.

The first one is the talk-to-the-star operation in which people pay $25 to $1000 per person for the opportunity to rub shoulders with someone famous.

At the second kind people pay a relatively small admission fee (say $5 per person) and there is a cash bar. This makes it possible for people with much less financial wherewithal to make a contribution to the campaign while at the same time enjoying themselves, a fundamental requirement of any fundraising event. (There is a certain strain of people on the left who like to be punished, and for those people you can create fundraising events at which they will be made to feel guilty and will not have a good time. This reinforces their sense of moral superiority, thus making it well worth a small investment in the admission fee.)

If it's possible for you to hold this type of cocktail party in a house which is well known for its beauty, its age, its garden and so on, some people will pay $5 or $10 merely to see the house.

The third type of cocktail party is the cocktail party for potential large contributors, at which no admission fee is required, but a pitch is made at some point during the evening.

There are several variations on these themes that you might try. A party for wealthy donors at $100 a couple (for congressional candidates) up to $1000 a couple (for presidential candidates) can be held earlier in the evening, to be followed three or four hours later by a more public rally at $5 a couple with a cash bar. Or to kick off a campaign with a lot of hoopla, you can set up a series of eight or ten parties in one night in a community, which the candidate can visit in the course of three or four hours.

There are other types of parties which should be tried, with the only limits being imagination and public decency. Wine-tasting parties have been used successfully in suburban liberal neighborhoods as a way of attracting people to make contributions of $5-$10 per person. Apple cider and donut parties at Halloween, New Year's Eve drop-in parties, or any type of parties that are done for pleasure can also be done for profit. In large cities, parties for singles can be very successful fundraisers, for people are often looking for ways to meet others who share a perspective on the world. Singles parties for candidates or causes fulfill that need.

DINNERS

Dinners are another traditional fundraiser. They normally require the presence of the candidate in a campaign situation or an outside national figure in a non-campaign situation.

Generally speaking, the small priced dinners ($10 a plate or less) are not worth the time and trouble involved as fundraisers (although they may be a valuable exercise in getting people together or honoring someone, and will have a small financial payoff). If a dinner is held in a big hotel, even with a cash bar, dinner will frequently cost $5-$10 or more per person. Add to that the cost in terms of time, mailings, telephoning, arrangements and so on, and the payoff in dollars and cents can turn out to be quite small. The same amount of energy used to simply ask people for $5 contributions results in a greater net to the organization.

Dinners for $20 a plate and up can turn out to be very lucrative, although you're talking about a very limited clientele. One way to up the ante is to make a pitch at the dinner. There are famous pitchmen around the country, one of whom is Assemblyman Willie Brown of California. The story is told that at the conclusion of a civil rights dinner, Brown asked all the ministers in the audience to come forward. All of them, of course, came up to the front, faces beaming. He lined them up on the front of the stage, and gave them collection baskets, telling the audience that the ministers would carry the baskets through the audience to collect contributions, since they were men above reproach. The ministers, of course, were pleased that they had been selected for this honor. Then Assemblyman Brown said, "In order to start the contributions, each of the ministers here is going to contribute ten dollars of his own just to show that it's starting off on the right foot." There was considerable coughing, embarrassment, nervousness, borrowing from other people, red faces. It was clear that the ministers had not expected it, but they had been so obviously pleased with their responsibilities that they couldn't refuse to pay ten dollars for the great privilege of collecting money from others.

It takes finesse to pull off fundraising like that, to work the emotions of the audience so that they both want to give and are moved by the spirit of the occasion to give more than they might have otherwise. Little guidance by anyone can be given on that subject, as it is unfortunately a matter of touch and feeling developed over a period of time.

EVENTS

Special events of various sorts are yet another way of obtaining contributions. Benefit performances by sympathetic groups or individuals, from rock groups to classical string quartets, from folk singers to poetry readers, are an ever-possible source of substantial money. Beware, however, of a benefit with a nationally-known performer—while this brings on visions of lollipops, the problems of such a concert are in many instances greater than the income you will receive. Original capital can run as high as $10,000 for promotional costs, performer transportation, arena rental and guarantees, and additional police and security forces (frequently charged to the promoters). With that sort of original investment of capital, a substantial organization is required to raise the front money with no guarantee of return. Additionally, multiple problems arise which are at least as serious as the raising of the original capital. It's frequently difficult, if not impossible, to break through the retinue of managers, promoters, hangers-on, exclusive contracts and so on to reach the performer. Having reached the person, finding a suitable time in their schedule which gives you both an advantageous date and time to prepare is unlikely. There are then the inevitable transportation delays, long-distance telephone calls, problems of pre-paid advertising, worries about ticket sales, and so on, to make concerts with more than a couple of thousand people very, very difficult.

During the winter of 1970 the Vietnam Moratorium held a benefit concert which was very successful both artistically and financially, but in the summer of 1970 concerts with equally good talent lost over $50,000 of the backer's money.

On the other hand, local groups are frequently much easier to reach, promotional costs are less, guarantees on the auditorium are much lower, security police are not needed, and ticket sales can be publicized by mail, small advertisements, or by word of mouth. It is possible with a much smaller expenditure of funds to have a respectable-sized audience and a good income from the benefit.

Another way to run a sort of pseudo-benefit is to go to potentially sympathetic coffeehouses, cafes, bars, and nightclubs that have entertainment and ask them to make one evening a benefit on your behalf. That way you avoid all the hassle and work and at the same time have a good profit.

Film festivals can play an instructive as well as a fundraising role, although their success for the most part is limited to college communities. However, you may be able to arrange with a local theatre showing a politically-oriented movie to contribute part of a night's proceeds to you in exchange for your efforts to fill the house for that showing.

Lectures can at times be profitable. Obviously, it's impossible for a candidate or an organization to charge for speeches during a campaign, but lecturing after the election may be an effective way to pick up campaign debts (especially if your candidate was elected). In non-campaign situations, an organization can sponsor honorarium lecturers for a fee.

Other fundraising events to try are sales of various sorts. Those great standbys of women's clubs the world over, the bake sale and the rummage sale, frequently produce a hundred or two hundred dollars. While this is not a monumental amount of money, it permits otherwise uninvolved people to feel that they are contributing in some way, and it's not to be forgotten that those small amounts of money may be escalated into larger fundraising events or may pay for staff time, advertisements, office space, or supplies. It's always possible to find someone in your group with previous experience in this type of organizing.

Another form of the same thing is the pancake dinner, the all-you-can-eat-for-$1.95 dinner, the food booths at the local carnival or the state fair —in short, the $1, $2, $3 type of event which can involve people in your organization and at the same time raise money.

PLEDGES AND CLUBS

While a single contribution of $100 sounds like a great deal, a pledge of $8 per month for a year makes it possible for people who otherwise could not make a $100 contribution to do so.

In some states, such as Colorado, the Century Club (all $100 contributors) has become the backbone of the Democratic Party. Lyndon Johnson (as is frequently true) discredited even the best of devices by creating a President's Club for $1000 contributors to his presidential campaign and his ongoing administration. The collection of people gathered at his club reads like a roster of

Washington special interests. It's not necessary to demean yourself to that extent in order to get people to contribute to clubs in small amounts. George McGovern's presidential campaign has shown conclusively that it's possible to form another type of President's Club of people with no special interest objectives but who share a concern about the issues. He has formed a club of people pledging to give $10 a month from the time of his announcement until the election. This base of support has made it possible for him to generate other money.

CONTRIBUTIONS IN KIND

Contributions in kind is another form of fundraising often as valuable as dollars and cents. It is frequently possible to obtain paper from the local paper dealer, the use of a mimeograph machine or Xerox machine from a copy supply company, telephone lines in the evening in a corporate office, the use of an empty office in somebody else's building, the use of tables and chairs from a church, now and then the loan of someone as a public service from a business firm to an organization on a six-month basis, and so on down to contributions of paper, clips, and pencils. Technically any contribution from a corporation to a political campaign is illegal, and you should check to make sure that it is the owner of the business that is making the contribution and not the business itself. However, it is very common to find large amounts of corporate investment, including the use of corporate air craft, WATS lines and personnel. It's virtually impossible for the Internal Revenue Service to trace such contributions, even though they may be more valuable than dollars, and must legally be reported as a contribution.

ADVERTISEMENTS

The most spectacular and well-known ads are those which have been run in the News of the Week in Review section of the Sunday *New York Times*. At a net cost of about $8,800 per page, the return has varied from as little as $3,000 or $4,000 (for ill-timed antiwar ads) to over $100,000 (for Biafra relief). Other fundraising advertisements have on occasion yielded equally good returns. For instance, an advertisement on the rather esoteric subject of growth in Colorado, published as a full-page advertisement in the *InterMountain Jewish News*, paid for itself while educating relatively large numbers of people.

There are three basic criteria for placing an ad: the medium, the appeal, and the placement and timing.

1. You must find the *medium* which best reaches your potential audience. For the antiwar movement, this has frequently meant the News of the Week in Review section of the Sunday *New York Times*, which appeals to and reaches an enlightened, liberal, national audience—in large part an audience with above-average income. It may, however, be the local labor newspaper which best reaches your audience. Determining specifically the audience you wish to reach and then finding the media which reaches it is an important beginning.

2. You must find the *appeal* which is the most effective to your selected audience while being honest to the cause which you advocate. It is silly to talk to a consumer-oriented audience about the morality of international affairs, when it is possible to talk to them honestly about the impact of those international affairs on consumer prices. It makes little sense to talk to students about the tax consequences of a particular weapon system rather

61

than the morality and long-term impact of militarism.

Once the basic appeal is decided, it is then important to use *attractive layout and effective language* in the ad. A local advertising firm sympathetic to your cause or candidate may be willing to do the ad for you, or individuals in advertising firms may be willing to do it on their own time. (Incidentally, if you can find a sympathetic advertising firm, they can reduce the cost of the ad to you by kicking back the placement fee which they are paid by the newspaper. This is usually fifteen percent of the total cost of the ad.) In general, the three criteria to look for in an advertisement are: (1) It must be attractive so that it draws a reader's attention, which is accomplished in large part by the effective use of white space; (2) the language of the copy must be as sprightly as possible, using short sentences and words with very specific meaning; (3) there must be a good return coupon asking people for information about themselves, their willingness to volunteer, and a space to mark contributions. (My feeling about contribution space is to leave a blank first, with a dollar sign in front of it, followed by three or four amounts in descending order, down to five dollars. For example: $_____, $100, $50, $25, $5.) Almost all newspapers will require the name of at least one individual on the ad, and whenever possible that should be an honorary chairman or other prominent person in the community.

3. The final basic criteria of advertising is the *placement and timing* of the ad. Experience of the Vietnam Moratorium showed that an ad run in the *New York Times* on Sunday morning reached a national audience, speaking to one group of people, and that the same ad run the following week in a

New York morning paper resulted in contributions from New York commuters, an entirely different group of people. This is basically a matter of knowing something about the community in which you work and the audience which you seek.

The timing of the ad is at least as important as its placement. When other important events or similar kinds of ads distract people's attention, the income from advertising will be reduced spectacularly. For instance, Christmas time is a particularly grim time to attempt to raise money in any way, and is overwhelmingly futile in the newspapers. The same timing problem holds in last minute advertisements before an election, that is, an advertisement on Sunday asking for funds for the election on Tuesday. People will not contribute at that point because they realize that the expenditures have been made, that their money will not arrive until after the election, and that their money will be essentially debt-paying money and not money to support a candidacy in action.

PERSONAL SOLICITATION

Finally, as a first and last resort, it is possible to go to direct solicitation.

It is the rare campaign which is less than fifty percent financed by large contributors, and they often donate up to ninety percent of the total. The most phenomenally unaverage campaign was probably that of George Wallace's in 1968. If his records can be believed, something in excess of ninety percent came in contributions of $50 and less.

Most of the people who have large amounts to contribute are well known on both the left and right, and it is extremely rare to find a wealthy, somewhat ideological person who hasn't been asked before. As a consequence, most names will come from previous efforts. You should attempt to get contributors lists from earlier campaigns, although this may be difficult because people with these lists are often quite possessive about them. You should definitely read the newspapers (including the society pages) and try by word of mouth to develop your own sources.

In approaching potential contributors, it may be useful to have a specific expense in mind. This is basically a matter of knowing what the person's special concerns are—if he's interested in television campaigning, you might ask him to pay for a five-minute or one-minute TV spot. This worked well in the 1968 McCarthy campaign, where people contributed $50 to finance a canvasser's room and board for ten days.

Contributors should be treated as people, and you should try to involve them as much as possible in the campaign. Many of them want to be deeply involved, to feel that they're a part of things, and are not being used simply for their money. Others, however, never want to hear from the campaign, and they'll certainly let you know this!

Three forms of personal solicitation are possible: Mail, telephone or telegraph, and direct.

1. A personal *letter* written either by the organizer of the effort, by the candidate of the campaign, or by a personal friend of potential contributors in support of the cause may yield substantial contributions. It has to be obvious to the recipient of the letter that he is not one of a mass mailing effort, that the letter was written and typed individually for him, that the need is urgent, and that the writer has been willing to give substantially of his time and effort and money—in short, that it's just not another hype.

2. Another direct solicitation method is the *tel-*

egram or *telephone*. This is a more urgent way of reaching people to whom you might write personal letters if time permitted, and is frequently used toward the end of a campaign to obtain the last needed burst of funds or when unexpected expenses (such as bail) arise. It is easy to send a large number of telegrams to potential contributors—you simply give the names and addresses with a message to the telegraph company, which will then send the message to any number of people. A night letter is also a method for quick delivery of a more extended message. The costs are obviously high, but because a sense of urgency and personal contact is conveyed by a telegram, the returns may be proportionately higher and will most assuredly be faster than by sending a letter.

The telephone is often used, most frequently in recent years in raising bail money on an overnight basis. My own experience has not been very good with telephone fundraising. Unless it is a clear one-time situation where money is needed quickly, people resent being contacted by telephone because it gives the impression that no one thought long enough to write a letter, and people object to contributing to what they regard as an inefficient organization.

3. The most difficult (and frequently the most successful) form of fundraising is the *personal visit*. No matter how it's said and how nice the people are to whom you're talking, there is always an element of being a mendicant, begging at the knees of those with money. I find the process degrading with people I dislike and very difficult with friends. The best rule that I know is to try not to solicit funds from people you like or think you might like on a personal basis. Unfortunately, in my experience this has never been possible. In the final analysis an organization is addicted to money and unable to survive without it. We all end up risking and straining friendships in an effort to preserve an organization. That's never been an equation I liked.

One way to avoid or at least lessen that strain is never to appeal for funds on the basis of friendship. When you must go to those people who are your friends, go to them with something which you know to be solid, responsible, important, and worthy of their support in some abstract sense— not worthy of their support merely because you are their friend.

The worst situation is to ask someone for money whom you know slightly or hardly at all and be turned down. No matter how well-intentioned they may be, it's very hard to forgive them for putting you in a situation where you are a beggar and they refuse to give a dime. The only worse experience is to have people make vast promises and then give only a pittance in comparison to their capacity to give. That is the only situation that leaves a more bitter taste than complete denial.

In any case, personal solicitation requires the presentation of a clear statement of what it is you intend to do, what it will cost and why, where the money will go, what other sources of funding you intend to develop, how you intend to kick the habit of asking rich people, the kind of staff you will be working with, and a clear projection of where you're going and what chances of success you will have. This is only the first step.

The second and most critical step is to appeal to the particular interests of the person to whom you speak. Sometimes that will be a highly ideological interest, a concern about morality in public affairs, or a commitment to a view of the world which you share. At times the appeal will be much more personal. It will require placing the contributor on a board of directors, dropping the contributor's name with friends in the press or not dropping the name with friends in the press, insuring that the contributor is invited to an event you may hold, convincing them that by donating money they will endear themselves to students the world over or to some other group the world over, and finally, most obvious but never said, the commitment in the case of a candidate that the contributor will always have an open telephone line and a receptive ear from the candidate if the election is successful. It is here that the possibility of making commitments which will later be regretted is greatest, and where the true relationship between money and politics becomes most obvious. Don't be surprised if in the urgency of the moment you find yourself making commitments which you later regret. Just remember and don't do it again.

3

THE PRESS*

"Say, ain't some of the papers awful gullible about politics? Talk about come-ons from Iowa or Texas—they ain't in it with the childlike simplicity of these papers."

GEORGE WASHINGTON PLUNKETT

*Much of the information in this chapter is based on a press manual prepared by Ted Johnson for the Vietnam Moratorium Committee. I am grateful to Ted for permission to use the material.

The most important thing to remember about dealing with the press is that you're really talking about working with human beings, and it's absurd to treat newsmen in the abstract, as if they were some sort of different creature. They are people who appreciate being treated honestly and decently and not being undercut or being told stories which later turn out to be untrue. They appreciate candor and are able to distinguish in most instances between a direct answer and a fudge around it. They will do what almost any person will do when someone is not telling them the truth: go and try to find out what it is for themselves, and then be angry at the person who originally lied to them, both for the lie and for thinking they were dumb enough to fall for it. They appreciate getting more than a cursory few minutes of someone's time, and they appreciate having their judgment respected. They appreciate being told when you think they're off base and complimented when you think they're right on it.

My own experience is that it makes no sense at all to attempt to mislead the press or to distort things, as they will almost invariably come back at you for the distortion and for being misled, and it will destroy your relationship with them for the future.

If, on the other hand, you're candid and honest with them, they will pay great heed to what you say in the future, even when it is difficult, complex, or controversial material.

An example of loss of credibility is the Student Mobilization Committee, which made totally fanciful crowd claims during marches and demonstrations when the police and the press were giving accurate and at times generous estimates. For instance, at the march on Washington in November

1969, the SMC was claiming over a million people in a crowd which even by the most generous private estimates of its supporters was 300,000 or 400,000. Once they claimed a million (I suppose as a leverage to push the press into saying 600,000) they lost all semblance of credibility.

There is no law that says you can't go out for a drink with a reporter, that you can't tell him or her about things you think are newsworthy, or that you can't attempt to cultivate his or her friendship. On the other hand, there is no law that says the reporter has to write all of what you tell, has to treat you fairly, or that the friendship of the barstool will carry over into news columns.

It won't take you long to distinguish between those reporters who are friendly or potentially friendly and those who regard their mission in life as an attempt to chop you apart. If you get harassed by a reporter, while you may have to find a way to cut that person off, sometimes the press will take care of their own. During the press conference on the first day of the Vietnam Moratorium, one reporter, Anthony Dolan from the *National Review,* insisted on asking every third question. The question was always the same · what about the telegram the Moratorium received from Ho Chi Minh? After four or five times of asking the question, a number of reporters suggested to him rather forcefully that they wanted to get information and they were tired of his harassing questions.

On occasion, of course, you come across that person who regards himself as a reporter of the news, who attempts as accurately as possible to convey what you said in either its brilliance or its stupidity, and to do the same for your opponents. These people are rare, and much to be valued.

In any case, journalists will respect you if you know something about their craft and attempt to provide them with the information they need in order to be good and accurate reporters of events.

In writing this chapter, I have assumed the most complex situation, and as a consequence you may find a great deal which is not relevant to you. For example, if you are in a city which has one weekly newspaper and two radio stations, you will rarely hold a full-blown news conference. However, you may on occasion prepare a news release. For others the most important section of this chapter may be that on interviews. Before getting to the role of the campaign or organization press person, a few notes on news may be helpful.

NEWS AND PUBLICITY

Sometimes events which might be seen as pure publicity and public relations gimmickry can be turned into legitimate news stories, and the difference, while a subtle one, is important. If you're to maintain a continuing relationship with the press over a period of time, they have to come to recognize that when you tell them that you have news, you actually do. Therefore it's dangerous and really destructive to try and portray as news those things which are not. A slightly different view of what might be a PR event, however, can make it into a legitimate news item. Shortly after the President's escalation of the war in April of 1972, a group in Denver, Colorado wanted to announce that they were seeking funds for refugee relief and to give an address where that money could be sent. However, since newspapers and television stations are generally not in the fundraising business for anyone except themselves, the group's press conference would have been seen simply as an attempt to use the news media as part of a fundraising campaign. However, by saying that the group was beginning a fundraising drive, and by having at that press conference someone who had recently been in Vietnam, it was possible to turn the group's announcement into a legitimate story about the refugee situation and the terrible need there, and, at the same time, to announce the fundraising drive. These subtle differences in the treatment of the situation transformed a PR gimmick into a legitimate news item—an important difference in maintaining relations with newspeople.

An important distinction to be kept in mind is between "hard" news and "soft" news. "Hard" news is that which is extremely urgent and significant and which is given prominent placement in newspapers, magazines and news broadcasts. "Soft" news is less urgent and significant and is placed less prominently in the media. Soft news stories are dispensable, and if space is needed for a late-breaking story, they will be removed. A deleted soft news item is rarely missed by the public; a hard news item surely would be. Feature stories, human interest articles, and some interviews are examples of soft news.

Abstract definitions of "publicity" and "soft" news are similar, and they are equally fuzzy in practice. A balance between hard and soft news will be sought by editors. Consequently, when you have saturated an area with hard news it may be possible to expand coverage with soft news.

Paid advertising (as opposed to a news item) is another way to convey a message through media. Anyone with a large amount to spend on advertising can hire a professional firm to prepare paid supplements for news coverage. One word of caution: every advertising person, whether hired or volunteer, will tell you that his themes and schemes are the only ones to carry the day. It is not necessarily true. Ask another ad person—you will receive another set of "the only way to win" ads. Once you have two sets you begin to suspect that there are others, and there are. A politically sophisticated individual in good touch with his real and potential constituency will have judgment every bit as good as (or sometimes better than) an equally good ad person. Hire an advertising firm if you can or must, but *do not be intimidated* into accepting anything your instincts warn you against.

The decision as to what information constitutes news is made on the basis of general and continuing interest (the war in Vietnam), urgency or excitement (crime), personalities (the Kennedys). strangeness (hippies), and difference of opinion (protest). Other contributing factors are the urgency of the news itself, the limitations of the particular news medium, and the amount of information available.

Obviously such complex judgments are not always accurate. Sometimes very significant stories are ignored because they were presented poorly to editors. Sometimes reporters simply do not know of the newsworthy information until too late. Other times, significant stories occur without reporters being prepared to cover them. For example, television must have a visual element for most of its news presentation. If its news bureau is not near the event, it will not be able to prepare filmed coverage, and will probably not broadcast the news.

The key to having your information judged favorably by editors is effective and professional presentation. Editors must be supplied with as much accurate information as possible; they must have time to pass judgment upon it and prepare it for their use. The only way you can insure coverage is by giving the media adequate advance notice of newsworthy events. The press secretary is responsible for coordinating these efforts.

As a rule, it is wise to assign one person from an organization to the job of press secretary. Reporters can then deal with someone who is prepared to help them and a good working relationship between press secretary and reporters can develop. This is important from the point of view of the press secretary, the organization, and reporters themselves.

Reporters must feel that the press secretary is their "Man (or Woman) on the Scene" and that the person will be open and honest with them. If you are the press secretary, you must think like a journalist, and have a good sense for what is news and for the critical facts and details of that news item. You must know the working details of a newsperson's job: when deadlines are; the nature of different publications; the staff of news outlets; and the process by which the newspaper or news show is put together.

Your primary operating assumption must be that news editors are confronted with a glut of information and that some of it will never get past their desks. Further, the news media are badly understaffed and if they do not recognize actual news it is usually because it was not presented in a way that made it stand out from the plethora of PR releases, corporate promotion notices, and just plain garbage which crosses their desks.

The job, then, is to present your information

succinctly, so that they can judge it quickly and add to the original material if necessary.

THE NEWS RELEASE

The news release is the standard tool of the press secretary and is a necessity in any situation where you are dealing with a group of newspeople. It is a news story written primarily for reporters, but prepared in such a way that it can be used in a newspaper verbatim. It is designed to convey detailed information to reporters for use in writing their own story, but it should possess the objectivity, brevity, thoroughness, and clarity of a good news article.

The news release can be used to tell the story of an event such as a news conference. In these cases, the reporter usually will have his or her own observations to add to the release. However, the release can also stand completely on its own—telling of plans, progress, statistics; supplying color; describing the activities of the staff of the organization; declaring support or an endorsement; and providing general background information.

Remember that the number of news releases received each day by news bureaus is usually many more than they can use. One release can be very easily lost, misdirected, or separated from its other pages. Some releases are not read at all by newspeople, most are merely scanned, and only a few are actually read in their entirety and a story written from them. Be aware of this when you write and distribute the release.

You must realize that many releases do not reach print simply because they were prepared improperly and were confusing rather than helpful to news people.

I've outlined the basic news release format and a sample is provided at the end of the chapter, to help you better understand its elements and how they fit together.

1. *Headings.* Legal size (8½ x 14) paper should be used for news releases, since more words can fit on a page and the need for collating is reduced. It is wise to have a printed masthead with the organization's name and address (preferably in some color ink other than black) so that the source of the release is easily identifiable. Quite often the letterhead stationery of the organization is used.

In the upper right hand corner of the release be sure to type:

For further information, contact ——
followed by the name of the press secretary with office and home telephone numbers. For filing and reference purposes, it is usually wise to date and number releases in sequence in the upper left corner beneath the masthead.

2. *Release dates.* The release date, the first line of the release, is probably the most important item for reporters second to the information itself. There are two basic forms for release dates:

```
For release upon receipt:
Tuesday, April 1, 1890

For immediate release:
Tuesday, April 1, 1890
```

These two indicate that the reporter can write the story as soon as the release is received. Sometimes urgency can be communicated by this type of release date. However, you should be aware that it can be a distinct disadvantage since it is unclear as to exactly when the story broke. For example, a release with this date sent out in the morning is geared primarily for afternoon papers. However, if its distribution is slow, it might miss most editions of that afternoon's paper. At the same time, it becomes old news for the morning newspapers of the next day and will not be used.

It is usually best to use a release date that has a specific time indicated for its release. This should be done when the release is distributed in advance of the release time. Newspeople will have ample time to consider it; can plan their story more thoroughly; and can get additional information if required. Most important, the information cannot be ignored by reporters because of late delivery or concern that it is old news.

There are many variations on this type of release date, all based on the deadlines of the news media:

```
For release in     ) For all morning
morning papers,    ) newspapers and
Tuesday, April 1   ) news shows

For release at     ) For use after
2 p.m.             ) that hour. Usual-
Tuesday, April 1   ) ly used because
                   ) it's the hour of
                   ) an event, such as
                   ) news conference,
                   ) which is subject
                   ) of release

For release on     ) Usually used for
or after           ) feature story
Tuesday, April 1   ) which is useful
                   ) over a period
                   ) of time
```

It is frequently necessary to indicate two release dates—one for newspapers and the other for radio and television. Usually this is done with extremely important information issued for Sunday newspapers. This practice allows the broadcast media to use it Saturday evening, since Sunday newspapers are often on sale by that time. A dual release date would be as follows:

> For release in morning papers
> Sunday, April 6
> For broadcast use after 6 p.m.
> Saturday, April 5

Be sure to remember deadlines when planning the release date. Remember especially that wire services must be able to use the information in time to get the news to newspapers before deadlines.

3. *Other structural matters.* Following the release date is the *headline*, which should be centered and typed in upper case letters. For example:

PLUNKETT BLASTS CIVIL SERVICE LAWS

If a dateline is needed to indicate the place and day the story originated, put it before the first paragraph of the release in the following form:

New York City; April 1, 1890

The body of the release should follow and at the end of each page should be typed:

MORE   (or)   .../

to indicate that there is another page.

On the top of each succeeding page the headline should be repeated together with the page number. Thus:

```
Plunkett Blasts Civil Service
       Laws....page 2
```

The end of the release should be indicated with:

```
END          (or)          -30-
```

placed at the very end of the release.

If there are attachments to the release, they should be itemized on the last page of the release itself. For example:

```
Attached: text of Plunkett statement.
```

If possible, provide the full text of letters, statements or relevant documents so that reporters are not dependent solely on the release for quotations and information.

4. *The style of the release.* The body of the release should be double spaced and printed on just one side of the paper. It should always be written in the past tense, as though the event has just occurred, even when a release is distributed before its release date.

If you've not had previous experience in writing news releases, take your local newspaper and study the style in which news stories are written. When writing your own release, try for conciseness and simplicity of expression, and don't be afraid to use your imagination. A good news story is one with enough information to make a person feel their time has been well spent reading it.

News stories are written in a style known as "pyramid"; it starts with the most significant facts and works down to the least significant. Theoretically this allows an editor to freely lop paragraphs off the end to fit the available space.

The first two paragraphs of a news release answer the questions who, what, when, how, and why. The verb of the first sentence should be strong and should indicate the major action: i.e. announced, denounced, urged, declared. The succeeding paragraphs then can supply additional information as needed, including if possible several quotes from identified spokesmen.

Use short declarative sentences, no more than three or four in a paragraph. Write "objectively," so that it could legitimately be printed verbatim in a newspaper without your biases being evident. If you want to present an opinion, quote someone as saying it.

5. *Broadcast problems.* In addition to the release, broadcast journalists may want a tape or news film to accompany their newscast. A news conference fulfills that need. However, if the release stands by itself, subsequent arrangements can be made for interviews of individuals.

One technique that can be tremendously effective in assuring coverage for your candidate or cause and in encouraging familiarity with your candidate's voice is the beeper phone—a simple device which allows you to feed audio material directly to radio stations. They are much more likely to use audio material than a written press release.

To rig up a beeper phone you need a cassette tape recorder and two alligator clips connected to the same plug. The male plug is plugged into the monitor socket on the tape recorder. The alligator clips are attached to the terminals which are revealed when the telephone mouthpiece is unscrewed.

Excerpt from your press release the most important part of the candidate or speaker's statement into a 40-60 second piece. Have the person read the statement into the cassette recorder, and then call radio station hot line numbers (a list of which should be kept handy) and tell them you have a radio feed from your headquarters.

When you call, have the feed's "in-cue" (the first four words) and "out-cue" (the last four words) plus the length of the piece ready for the station. They will tell you when to go and you simply play the tape for them. When you have the beeper set up, you have to press the "record button" on the tape recorder and talk through the microphone in order to talk to the radio station.

The phone beeper gives radio stations live feeds to play throughout their news cycle, often the only live feed that the radio station will have except the announcer.

In the case of rallies, major speeches, or news conferences, always tape the speech, including the question and answer period. Then you can treat it as you would a press release radio feed. Save the tape from the question and answer session to feed to radio stations on slow news days.

The third use of a beeper phone is for candidate or organization response to developing situations. Radio is obviously a very current media and you have to be quick to get coverage. If shortly after any major announcement, you give a feed on policy shift or question of public interest on which your candidate or organization has a strong position, radio stations will use it to fill out their news stories.

THE PRESS STATEMENT

The press statement is used to provide news people with a statement by an organization or its leaders without additional comments and background material. It is intended to be a complete statement and is presented to reporters in its entirety. (It may, however, also be used to supplement a press release.)

The form of a press statement is similar to a release, including a release date. The headline should read:

STATEMENT BY CITIZENS FOR CLEAN GOVERNMENT

This should be followed by a short introductory sentence giving the circumstances of the statement. For example:

> The following is a statement of
> Citizens for Clean Government in
> response to G.W. Plunkett's denun-
> ciation of civil service reforms.

The statement should follow, set off in quotation marks or indented from both margins.

A press statement can also be used on the beeper phone, or called in to newspapers provided the statement is timely and short. Calling conveys a sense of urgency and increases the likelihood of its use. Do this, however, only if there is no other way to get the statement to the news agencies in sufficient time.

THE PRESS KIT

A press kit is simply a collection of documents or materials in a pocket folder. It is used for two purposes: first, as background material about your organization or your candidate, to be kept on hand at all times; second, for a major press conference or an event. It may include fact sheets, biographical information on individuals, photographs, reprints of newspaper articles and speeches, and whatever other materials may seem appropriate. Be sure the folder is adequately labelled for quick identification.

THE FEATURE STORY

The feature story is prepared in much the same way as a release but is generally less timely and urgent than hard news. It can be about people, office, staff, neighborhood studies, items of human interest, or colorful aspects of the campaign or organization.

Feel free to ignore the rigid pyramid style of hard news when writing a feature story. A catchy or provocative opening is good, followed by lively and imaginative development of the story. It's not at all necessary to state all the basic information in the first few paragraphs—in fact, the story will probably read better if you don't.

You write a feature story for two basic reasons: first, newspeople often do not have the time to research and write such a story, but will be anxious to adapt one; second, reporters may get an idea of their own from the story. Local radio and TV stations should also receive feature material on the off chance that it may stimulate a news idea.

Because local television stations often use feature stories to fill holes in their evening news programs, it is a very good idea to let the stations know when your group or candidate is doing something that would make a good film story. Often these kinds of events will not make news in the newspapers but, because of the color or uniqueness of the situation, television will pick it up.

Remember not to neglect photographers. When a good visual event that's light on hard news is coming up, always be sure to notify the newspaper and wire service photographers. A picture may not be worth a thousand words, but it does remind the public that you're around.

MEMORANDUM TO REPORTERS

A tool used to inform reporters of practical matters and to supply them with information which is not intended for publication is the memorandum. The press secretary should carefully avoid use of release date or anything else which might lead news people to think that the material is for use as news.

The memorandum might be used to advise the press of a procedure for obtaining press credentials for an event, the likelihood of a future news conference, the appointment of a press secretary, or a change in plans.

INTERVIEWS

For some reason, reporters will often ignore releases and other prepared materials in order to get the same information by interview. Interviews can be an effective means of sending information to newspeople. You should feel free to suggest a topic and person for an interview to a specific reporter at any time you think such an interview would be appropriate and beneficial to your cause. In most cases, the candidate and his or her family or a leader of the organization is the obvious choice for an interview. However, particularly for a feature-type interview, an interesting individual who is not a leader can be suggested.

Always choose a representative who is reasonable, articulate and fully understands the organization and its activities. Be honest and open, while at the same time careful of what is said. The phrasing of an answer is very important. Most of us are sloppy in conversation and constantly modify or qualify our statements with tone of voice or expression. When the words are reduced to print such modification is gone and the stark reality of the words is often shocking. The person being interviewed should prepare by thinking out possible questions and framing answers to them.

It is surprising to see what happens to an individual when confronted with a microphone. Some perfectly articulate people "freeze," others blossom. You can't know until it happens. The first time you work with an individual it may be either a pleasant surprise or a minor disaster. The element of suspense may make life more interesting but you should be prepared to react quickly and help smooth over rough spots with ease and surety. It only happens once per new person.

THE NEWS CONFERENCE

A news conference is used to present specific major information to newspeople and to provide an immediate opportunity to respond to their questions and requests for additional information. It assures that the information will be given to all news media equally and simultaneously, and gives the electronic media a visual element for its newscasts.

If, however, the information could be presented as effectively with a release, do not waste the time of reporters. News conferences should be used *very sparingly* and only when there is some item of particular and urgent interest to convey. Don't let yourself get into a situation where the press gets your notice of a conference and says, "Oh, another one of those," and doesn't bother to come.

Use your imagination in choosing a setting for the conference. Remember that news conferences do not always have to be dull, dry events held in hotel meeting rooms. When Senator Fred Harris introduced legislation to break up shared monopolies, it wasn't from the floor of the Senate—he used the steps of the General Motors headquarters in New York City as his platform. The setting alone gave color and life to the issue he was discussing and it provided great visuals for television.

Not all issues lend themselves to this kind of treatment, but many do if you use your imagination in deciding how to dramatize the issue and maximize press coverage. If your candidate or group is attacking a local corporation that is polluting the town's river, don't launch your attack from a hotel room. Go to the river and let the television cameras film the refuse gushing from the factory.

Arrangements. The news conference should be carefully planned in advance. Use a room which is well lighted and adequate in size for the number of reporters you expect. A conference room, such as that in a hotel, is usually best suited for a formal conference. Be sure that the room is not too big for your anticipated attendance. If you're just starting up in the community, you may want to have the conference in your new office as tangible proof you're actually in business and operating.

The physical arrangement for the room should be in arena style, with a head table facing rows of chairs for reporters with an adequate center access aisle. Ample space should be provided behind the rows of chairs for television lights and cameras. However if speakers talk from a seated position, the cameras must sit to either side of the reporters, so you'll have to provide room for them accordingly.

Ideally speakers should address the gathering from behind a lectern placed on the head table. A lectern gives the audio technicians a place to situate their microphones. In less formal conferences, it may be possible to move microphones from person to person sitting at the head table, but such an arrangement can be awkward and potentially confusing if not well planned.

A word of caution: TV reporters quite often will try to take over a conference by removing the newspaper reporters' chairs from the front of the room and putting their cameras there. *Don't let this happen.* When the problem comes up, politely, but firmly tell the TV people to leave the chairs in front. Don't be intimidated by the sight of their cameras and electronic equipment. The success of the conference depends greatly in your ability to establish and maintain control of the situation.

Coffee and perhaps pastry should be provided for reporters along with ice water for those at the head table.

Non-newspeople occasionally are invited to attend news conferences as guests. This is done to reward volunteers, to make a pitch to contributors, or simply to insure having a responsive audience for the information being presented. Such a practice is acceptable so long as it does not go to extremes. The press conference is meant to supply information to reporters and anything that impedes this process is not desirable. Therefore, invite a few guests or supporters if you wish, but only to observe. Do not direct remarks to them or permit them to ask questions in competition with reporters. They should never respond to the questions of reporters, unless specifically asked to do so.

All speakers should remain at the head table throughout the entire conference. Allow adequate space behind the table for speakers to move easily from their seats to the lectern, if one is used.

Notification of reporters. The news conference should be announced as far in advance as possible: three or four days is sufficient time. Notify all reporters and members of the broadcasting and TV media first in writing, followed by a phone call to each person to make sure they received the release.

The phone call is important for it provides an opportunity to indicate the importance of the conference and to convince the reporter to attend.

You can use the telephone call to discuss the subject of the conference in more detail. Be sure to note, however, that the material is not for release until the news conference. Be certain to repeat the date, time, place, and speakers during the conversation.

Headline your written notification

NOTICE OF A NEWS CONFERENCE

In chart form give the date, time, place, speakers, and general subject. When indicating the subject provide only a sketch in very general terms without many details. The purpose of the notice is to attract interest—not to tell the whole story. Briefly indentify the speakers and state that there will be time for questions and answers. Be sure you clearly indicate who should be contacted for further information. If speakers are able to stay afterward for private interviews, state this as well.

The wire services in some cities provide a date book listing events for reporters. Be sure to find out if they maintain such a book and advise them of the conference, listing full details, in addition to notifying a reporter from the wire service.

News release for a news conference. Prepare a thorough news release for distribution at the conference. Summarize the information presented at the conference; put it in perspective; name and identify speakers; and supply quotes from each speakers' prepared remarks.

Arrange a meeting with the speakers a day or two before the conference to plan the conference itself and to map out their individual statements. With this information, writing a release that will conform to what is said at the conference is a simple matter.

If there are several documents for distribution at the conference in addition to the release, a press kit should be prepared. If speakers present prepared statements, provide them in press statement form. Hand out all documents to reporters as they arrive so they may look it over and plan their questions. Be sure to get the names of all reporters and their affiliation as they enter the room. Locating a table for this purpose just inside the door makes the job easier.

News conference format. It is usually unwise to have more than two speakers for a news conference. One exception to the two-person rule may be a newly-founded community group which wants to show that it has a broad and diversified base of support, and hence may have four or five speakers representing different ethnic, racial, economic, or professional groups.

Opening statements by each of the speakers should be limited to three or four minutes apiece.

Move as quickly as possible to the question and answer part of the news conference, for it is often the most important in terms of lively news copy.

The news conference should start late to allow for late arrivals, but should never be delayed more than ten minutes.

Do not start the conference slowly or accidentally. When it is time to begin, have all the speakers at the front of the room ready to take their places behind the head table. Introduce each speaker by his or her full name, speaking directly into the microphones. Complex last names should be spelled out. Then explain the format of the conference, indicating the order in which people will speak and specify that there will be time for questions and answers afterwards.

It is unnecessary for the press secretary to remain at the head table, although it should be clear that the press secretary is running the press conference. In addition to planning it, the press secretary starts it, keeps it going and, if necessary, ends it. Sometimes, however, the reporters themselves will stop the conference after a period of time. If they do not, one of the speakers or the press secretary should stop the press conference by thanking the reporters for their attendance. Do this when it seems that the purpose of the conference has been served. Good press conferences should last *no longer than thirty minutes*.

Following the press conference reporters may seek interviews with individual speakers. Be fair with regard to these interviews: if one reporter has a chance to interview a speaker then all reporters should have the same opportunity. You do not have to offer the opportunity, but be cooperative if it is asked for.

News conferences should be taped by you so that you have a record of what is said. You can then answer questions of who said what and supply direct verbatim quotes if they are needed. In addition, reporters unable to attend the conference can be provided with the full transcript of what occurred.

Immediately after the conference, deliver the conference releases to those newspapers and radio and TV stations not in attendance, and call in taped excerpts to the radio stations on your phone beeper. These additional steps help to insure coverage by all the media in your area.

EVENTS

When public speeches, rallies or demonstrations are held, be sure to give adequate and complete notice to reporters. Provide them with releases or kits containing information, texts of speeches, and biographical information. Be close to reporters all through the event to provide information, and be certain you know everything there is to know about it. A press section, a press room, or tent with telephones and typewriters should be provided when necessary or possible. If you can arrange a press briefing immediately before the event with all major participants in attendance, it is extremely helpful to reporters.

WEEKLY NEWSPAPERS

There are a large number of less-than-daily publications. Most of these have a locality, a neighborhood, or defined community (such as a college campus) as their audience. Since these publications cannot compete with the daily media for hard news, they are often good outlets for the features and special interest stories. Since these publications are frequently one-person operations, they have a greater need for prepared stories, such as releases and features, which are in a form ready for insertion in the publication.

Know the deadlines of these publications so that an editor can be alerted to a hard news item which suits his schedule. If you release information on a day the publication is issued, the editor should be given the information in advance so he can use it. This often results in front page placement of the story, and should be a consideration in choosing the day to release information.

Most important in dealing with publications of this sort is to provide information which is not the warmed-over leftovers from the daily media. Give them a feeling that their audience, whether students or small-town residents, is important to your organization or candidate, and they'll give you good coverage.

CALENDARS

Many newspapers and radio stations maintain and supply a calendar listing of activities in the community. It is very simple to call them, find out who handles the calendar, determine what the publication wants, and then provide that information.

PUBLIC SERVICE ANNOUNCEMENTS

By law, radio and television stations must allot a certain amount of time to public service announcements. This means that the station broadcasts material which is prepared and supplied at no cost to the station. Some stations will only accept material from non-profit and non-political sources. Check with the station's public service director to determine what is acceptable.

There are two ways to use this time. The first is to prepare a script which discusses an activity of the organization. The announcement should be typed in uppercase letters and triple spaced. It should be carefully written to conform with the reading length specified by the station, usually 20, 30, or 60 seconds. For television announcements, several pertinent 2x2 transparencies should accompany the script to provide a visual element.

The second use of public service time is to provide mass-produced tapes to the station. Various national organizations, such as Business Executives Move for Vietnam Peace, are now producing issue-oriented tapes for this purpose in varying lengths, including some of program length. Get a sample from one of these organizations and take it to the public service director of a station. If he or she is willing to use it, it should be provided without cost. If it is refused, there is no way to compel a station to use the material.

TALK SHOWS

Talk shows are free media, and give you exposure that otherwise would cost money. Make every effort to get qualified representatives onto talk shows and to call into talk shows since they often have a large and devoted listening audience.

Arranging for representatives of a visible and active organization to appear on television or radio talk shows is usually not too difficult. Choose a person who is articulate, a good conversationalist, has a sense of humor and is well versed on the organization, its rationale, and its activities. Contact the person at the station responsible for the show and suggest the guest and a topic of discussion. When a decision is made by the station, confirm it as soon as possible. Send material on the organization and a biographical sketch of the guest so that the show's staff may prepare for the program beforehand. Be sure to find out where, when, and to whom the guest should report. Remember that some shows are taped well in advance of presentation.

Help the guest prepare for the show by thinking of possible questions and helping frame answers to them. The guest should have several points to make and should be aware of possible opportunities to make them. Thus the guest can "plug" the date and place of an activity or program. For this to be done unobstrusively it needs to be well thought out in advance.

You may be asked to provide a panel instead of one guest. Other times, a person of the opposite point of view may be desired for a debate. Feel free to do as you wish, but remember that exposure for the organization is helpful no matter what the circumstances. The one exception to this is the "insult" talk shows, which should be avoided. There's no sense in spending your time, or anyone else's time, being kicked around by the local demagogue.

Some talk shows have a phone-in format whereby guests can be questioned by members of the listening audience. If you have a guest on such a show, try to arrange for supporters to call in, so long as the result is not too obviously contrived. Also, if you know of a guest from another point of view on a show, arranging for phone calls to that person can give your organization exposure.

Keep a file on local talk shows including the time and frequency of broadcast, whether the show is live or taped, the time of taping, who to contact, and the type of audiences they reach.

GENERAL MATTERS

Lists of Newsmen

You must keep accurate and up-to-date lists of publications, contacts, and reporters. A file should be maintained by categories of publications, and by reporters. One publication may appear in several categories, but with different persons specified and for different purposes.

In the reference section of a library, you will find various directories, organized by area or nationally which list the staff of news outlets, and from which your lists can be compiled. The best known national directories are *Editor and Publisher, Broadcasting Yearbook, Ayer and Son Directory, Working Press of the Nation.* Turn-over of staff in most news agencies is high, so make every effort to keep your lists up to date. Of course, the names and addresses of local media can be obtained from the telephone book, and you can call a newspaper or broadcast outlet to find out the name of a particular editor or reporter.

Watch newspaper by-lines and news programs so that you can add to your list reporters who specifically cover issues related to your organization. Frequently reporters who cover you once will ask to be sent material in the future and should be added to the lists.

A system of file cards is the best way of maintaining these lists. A typical card might look like this:

```
NEW YORK HERALD TRIBUNE
100 West 43rd Street          399-6215
New York, New York

                    Contact: Wm. L. Riordon

5-9:  Attended news conference
5-12: Interviewed G. W. Plunkett
```

How to use a press list

Send only one copy of a release to each news agency. If additional back-up copies are sent, be sure to note the others on an attached sheet of paper. It is a good idea to send a back-up copy to the city desk or to the city editor in case the reporter who got the primary copy is doing another story or is out of town. If the release is not sent to a specific reporter at a news outlet, then the primary copy should be sent to the city editor.

Particularly significant releases can also be sent to non-reporters, such as columnists, editorial writers, and producers of talk shows. In such cases, the recipients should know that you do not expect them to write a news story. The best way to communicate this is by writing "For Your Information" across the top of the release.

Releases can be distributed by messenger or mail. Generally, considerations of time and expense determine the means to be used. It is best to distribute the release in person since it gives you an opportunity to convince reporters of the significance of the release and to supply additional information.

Feel free to ask the city desk or news desk who should be notified of a certain news item. Asking is better than blundering in the wrong direction.

Exclusives

As a general rule, the practice of giving information to a particular reporter or publication exclusively is not a good idea, and can prove to be a dangerous practice. It is unfair to the majority of reporters with whom you deal, and they may justifiably resent it. There are, however, several distinct advantages to the practice. Usually a newspaper will give more attention and better placement to a story which is exclusive with that paper. Interest in this story can sometimes be generated among other publications if it first appeared as an exclusive in one outlet. An exclusive can also be a way to pay a favor to a reporter who has been particularly helpful in the past.

As a rule, the unfairness of the practice overshadows all advantages. If a reporter uncovers the story, however, there is nothing to prevent it being run as an exclusive, except to release it quickly to all media. Usually it is just best to let the story break on its own. That way you reap the benefits of an exclusive without any of the disadvantages.

Bear in mind another type of exclusive which does not have the disadvantages described above. This is one which is directed to a specific type of publication, such as weekly newspapers or student newspapers. However, in such a case, the release should be headed:

EXCLUSIVE TO WEEKLY NEWSPAPERS

above the release date, to distinguish it from your general press release.

Off-the-record

Basically, nothing is "off-the-record" when given to a reporter. It is unrealistic to expect anyone—especially a reporter—to forget something they have been told. Thus, if something is secret and you want to keep it that way, do not tell it to a reporter. Wait until it can be discussed openly and completely.

On the other hand, the technique of discussing something "off-the-record" can be helpful to everyone concerned, providing it is opinion and background being discussed rather than facts. In these circumstances, a conversation "off-the-record" is one that will not be quoted. The reporter may allude remotely to the conversation, but will not quote it or paraphrase it. It will be regarded as speculation rather than news. The reporter, however, is able to get the full picture with all the background needed.

There is yet another technique which is frequently used by government officials. This is a conversation "not for attribution" in which the reporter may quote the individual providing that person is not identified. This technique is of little use to the campaign or citizens' organization and should be avoided.

I've put together some random notes in dealing with the press, all of which are proven by experience and all or some of which may be helpful to you. They all relate to one central thought—news people are human too and like to be treated that way.

Be accessible to reporters. Be available in person and by telephone, and always return calls promptly. Make a reporter feel welcome to stop in the organization's office for a chat and to see what is happening.

It is acceptable to use newspeople as resource persons for the organization. *Ask their advice,* ask them to be speakers at events. (Frequently they will refuse, but it doesn't hurt to ask.)

Send a memo of introduction to reporters when you have a regular person to work with the press.

Be respectful of the reporters' jobs. They are usually busy, so *don't waste their time* with idle conversation. If they want an in-depth discussion, give it to them. If not, keep your remarks short and to the point.

Work closely with the person in charge of scheduling for your candidate. Creative scheduling leading to colorful and interesting events can do more to get press coverage for your candidate than anything else you can do.

Be sure of the *importance of the story*. Do not try to exaggerate the significance of information.

Be sure of the *facts*. Check out *all details before* presenting them to reporters.

Do not be ashamed to admit that you do not have certain information. Try to get it to reporters as quickly as possible.

Follow the media which cover the activities of the organization or candidate so that you can know what's being said. If there is a clipping service for newspapers in your state, subscribe to it.

Don't be intimidated by the media. Remember that no reporter will ignore someone who can supply newsworthy information. But also remember that the reporter has a job to do. If the press secretary can help, fine. If not, he or she can prove to be a nuisance and do your cause more harm than good. Once reporters learn that a press secretary can be trusted they will work closely with that person.

I have purposely ignored the political problems you can potentially have with the media, and have assumed that the media is generally going to be open to the type of information your organization has to present. Unfortuntely this is not always the case. You may find a complete blackout of news on your organization. While I can offer no solution to this problem short of publishing one's own newspaper (not really a far-out idea), I can offer a bit of advice. Find out if the news blackout pervades all the media. If not, direct your news toward those outlets which will use it with the hope that others will follow as a matter of necessity. Seek out sympathetic reporters who are willing to write about the organization but whose editors will not print the story. Get their advice and try types of stories they think might pierce the blackout. Above all, be persistent. Keep talking to the media, but try to be as reasonable and as low-key as possible. Provide them with few excuses to avoid printing news about your organization.

In a situation which is really critical (i.e. it's impossible to get around some of the press by going to the other press people and impossible to find alternative media) try to create a national story about the news blackout. Newspeople are extremely sensitive to investigation by other newspeople. If it's possible to "point-a-finger" and to document adequately a news blackout of a genuine story, frequently the national press will be interested in that. It many even bring the local press around.

Have information. A press secretary without information is a contradiction in terms. Do not expect that information will always automatically come to you; look around for stories about the organization or campaign to develop for the press.

Use imagination and common sense!

EXAMPLE OF NEWS RELEASE

COMMITTEE FOR G. W. PLUNKETT

Tammany Hall
New York, N.Y.

(2) Number 12   (3) For further information,
                            contact: Chester Hyde
(4) For release at 2 p.m.   593-2957 (o)
     Tuesday, April 1, 1890   533-0019 (h)

(5) PLUNKETT BLASTS CIVIL SERVICE REFORM LAWS

(6) <u>George Washington Plunkett,</u> Tammany Hall
candidate for President, (7) <u>today</u> (8) <u>denounced</u>
(9) <u>civil service laws,</u> terming them <u>"the big-</u>
<u>gest fraud of the age, the curse of the nation."</u>
     "You hear of this thing or that thing
going wrong in the nation, the state, or the
city," he charged, speaking from his (11) <u>cam-</u>
<u>paign headquarters, the shoeshine stand in New</u>
<u>York.</u> "Look down beneath the surface and you can
trace everything wrong to civil service. The
civil service humbug is undermining our insti-
tutions, and if a halt ain't called soon this
great republic will tumble down like a Park
Avenue house when they were building the subway,
and on its ruins will rise another Russian
government."
 (12) <u>Plunkett called for a bipartisan approach</u>
<u>to the problem, advocating that "all the leaders</u>
<u>of the two parties should get together and make</u>
<u>an open, non-partisan fight against civil ser-</u>
<u>vice, their common enemy.</u>

(13) <u>- more -</u>

"The time is fast coming," he said, "when civil service or the politicians will have to go, and it will be here sooner than they expect if the politicians don't unite, drop all them minor issues for a while, and make a stand against the civil service flood that's sweeping over the country like them floods out West."

Plunkett, a long-time critic of civil service, said his opposition stems in part from concern for the youth of the country. "I have good reason for saying that most of the anarchists in this city today are men who ran up against civil service examinations," he said. "There was once a bright young man in my district who tackled one of these examinations. The next I heard of him he had settled down in Herr Most's saloon smoking and drinking beer and talking socialism all day long. Before that time he had never drank anything but whiskey. I knew what was coming when a young Irishman drops whiskey and takes to beer and long pipes in a German saloon.

"That young man is today one of the wildest anarchists in town," he said. "And just to think! He might be a patriot but for that cussed civil service.

"How are you going to interest our young men in their country if you have no offices to give them when they work for their party?" he queried.

(15) - 30 -

(16) Attached: text of Plunkett statement

1. Masthead

2. Release number

3. Who should be contacted for further information

4. Release date

5. Headline

6. Who

7. When

8. Strong verb—indicates what is dominant action in story

9. What

10. Why

11. Where

12. How

13. "—more—" or "... /" indicates that there is another page

14. Headline repeated with page number

15. "—30—" or "END" indicates the conclusion of the release

16. Statement indicating that documents are attached

4

SCHEDULING, ADVANCE, AND RALLIES

"The very constitution of the Tammany Society requires that we must assemble at the wigwam on the Fourth, regardless of the weather, and listen to the readin' of the Declaration of Independence and patriotic speeches.

"You ought to attend one of these meetin's. They're a liberal education in patriotism. The great hall upstairs is filled with five thousand people, suffocatin' from heat and smoke. Every man Jack of these five thousand knows that down in the basement there's a hundred cases of champagne and two hundred kegs of beer ready to flow when the signal is given. Yet that crowd stick to their seats without turnin' a hair while, for four solid hours, the Declaration of Independence is read, long-winded orators speak, and the glee club sings itself hoarse.

"Ah, that is the highest kind of patriotism, the patriotism of long sufferin' and endurance."

GEORGE WASHINGTON PLUNKETT

SCHEDULING

Scheduling is closely tied to campaign strategy. As a consequence, only general rules can be given since strategy will, in substantial part, determine where and how the time of the candidate is spent.

In recent campaigns, it has become vogue to use crowds, even at the senatorial and congressional levels, primarily as a backdrop for media. A situation is created in which the candidate is seen as the choice of the screaming masses in the hopes that the image conveyed through television news film will make him the choice of the non-screaming masses as well. While this may be a clever use of people, I suspect it is one which is frequently resented, and will be increasingly resented as people become more aware of the way in which they're being used—not as a sounding board for the candidate's ideas or even for potential voters to be reached, but simply as bodies to be seen on television. Cleverness and contrivance can frequently have tremendous backlash potential. In any case, it seems to me unconscionable to create a circumstance where all scheduling is dictated by the media.

With that rather harsh warning, the other side of the picture is that there are media events which are highly beneficial for the candidate and the people involved. Factory handshaking was being done before television came out to film it at six o'clock in the morning, and it is still a legitimate way of meeting people, giving them a chance to meet you, and perhaps saying more than good morning as they pass by. Events should become opportunities to educate not only the people being met by the candidate, but the candidate as well. One of the most effective means of achieving this mix is by meeting people in their everyday surroundings. Certainly John Kennedy was a different and better man for his West Virginia campaign, where he came to see and feel compassion for the situation of the coal miner. The same is true of George McGovern in 1972, who in the early primaries had an opportunity to see in depth into the lives of people all over the country in a way that only a presidential candidate in the context of a campaign can see. He came away with a new understanding of how people live, and a new insight into their needs.

So with the caveat that cleverness can backfire, and gimmickry unrelated to substance has no place in a campaign, it is possible to outline a few rules, or at least ideas, for scheduling a candidate.

First, in a campaign where there's low name recognition, the early use of the candidate's time should be to build as broad a volunteer base as is possible. Time should be spent working with the greatest potential sources of volunteers—college communities, old age homes, and high schools.

Second, use of the candidate's time early in the campaign should be directed to work in his areas of greatest potential voter strength, particularly if it's a primary election.

Third, having built a base of support, you can then reach out to a larger constituency, and use the candidate's time to develop strengths in those areas of weakness. For instance, it would be beneficial for workers to see that a peace candidate is concerned about the circumstances in which they live and work. It is necessary to cover your tracks with a number of diverse constituencies in order to assure people that you are concerned about them, their lives, and their votes, and that you are willing to spend time listening and talking to them. Otherwise, your candidate may be branded as representing only a specific segment of the community. This is precisely what happened to Eugene McCarthy in 1968, when he was characterized as a candidate of the white upper-middle-class who didn't care about black votes. This was certainly not true, but it was the result of unbalanced scheduling.

Two additional observations may be helpful. First, whenever possible attempt to conserve the time of both the candidate and the campaign by using automatic crowds to present the candidate's message. To spend a great deal of time building a crowd in one place when a crowd of similar size and composition may be automatically available at a slightly different time and place is both absurd and it is wasted energy. For instance, to put together a meeting of your candidate's supporters on a college or high school campus is a waste of time when an all-school assembly may be available to the candidate. To try to build a crowd for a rally at a high school gymnasium is senseless when at the same time a shopping center in the area may already have hundreds or even thousands of people readily available and may also have facilities for a walking tour or speech. Conserve the energy of the campaign for building crowds in areas where automatic crowds are impossible, and when the extra expenditure of effort will reap guaranteed benefits.

Second, attempt not to exhaust the candidate intellectually as well as physically. Hubert Humphrey is touted as a great campaigner because he's up early in the morning and stays up late at night and seems to work hard in between. However, if your words have disintegrated into platitudinous mush, and you haven't the time to prepare thoughtful statements of value both to the community, to the people to whom you speak, and to the media, you're wasting your time and everybody else's time. Give the candidate time to think and reflect, and to build strength for important events.

There will be tremendous pressure for the candidate to attend even the smallest event, and of course you don't want to deny people the opportunity to meet the candidate. But don't deplete the very strength which made your candidate in the first place, which hopefully is intellectual capacity, reflective ability, willingness to listen, and decisiveness.

Ultimately, there is only one rule in scheduling —use imagination. Using the front door of one of your opponent's chief supporters, as Jess Unruh did in California in the 1970 gubernatorial election, may be controversial but it attracted widespread attention to the issues of an irresponsive, irresponsible tax structure and a governor bound into a small group of very wealthy interests.

Admittedly, it is harder for a candidate supporting the status quo to use much imagination, but then those who support the status quo tend to have very little imagination anyway, so there's not much lost.

ADVANCE

Advancing has in recent years become a rather glorified profession, largely thanks to Jerry Bruno, who has used the advance person's role as a base for political organizing.

The substantive principles of advance work are very simple. The advance person is the candidate's representative on the scene before an event, responsible for both political and logistical arrangements for the event, and responsible for every detail involved with a successful appearance. Obviously this is a highly specialized professional task at the level of presidential campaigns and even in some large senatorial campaigns, although it is not always done well.

In the 1972 presidential campaign when Eugene McCarthy actively entered only the Illinois primary, he had working for him an advance man who had formerly worked for Hubert Humphrey. Senator McCarthy had given a speech in Iowa on a weekday evening, and was scheduled for a morning arrival in Chicago. The advanceman ran from the hotel, jumped into a car which he assumed was one of the cars rented to the campaign, and took off for O'Hare Airport. It was soon discovered that a private car had been stolen from the hotel's carport, and an all points bulletin was issued for the arrest of the person driving that car. In addition, the advanceman arrived at the airport a few minutes before the plane was to arrive to discover that Senator McCarthy had flown into Midway Airport rather than O'Hare. The Senator, finding no one there to meet him, simply caught a taxi to the hotel. All in all a classic of advancing ineptitude.

At its most professional, advancing requires pedantic and compulsive attention to detail, the imagination of a political organizer, and tremendous persistence. Its main ingredients are the willingness to carry through and a substantial degree of common sense. If you have people in the campaign who possess those characteristics, you can use them to insure that the candidate is not scheduled into halls that are too big; into consecutive events that are much further apart than it's possible for him to drive; to speak to hostile crowds unprepared; or left standing at a rally without adequate speaker equipment.

I am assuming that in most campaigns where this manual will be useful the candidate will be speaking primarily to automatic crowds and that the substance of advance work will be handled by the scheduler, who will insure that preparations for the candidate's presence, and his political homework are completed.

RALLIES

The organization of rallies is a more common experience, one that campaign and noncampaign organizations share, and the same elements of organizing apply in either instance. These elements fall into three basic categories: choosing the site, building the crowd, and the rally itself.

The first consideration is finding a place with a built-in crowd and preferably one with symbolic importance. Occasionally it will be both necessary and possible to build a crowd for a rally at a relatively out-of-the-way place if you have an issue of intense local interest or a well-known national figure scheduled to speak.

A prime consideration should be accessibility and size of the location (large enough to look respectable, but under no circumstances so large as to dwarf the crowd). A realistic, as opposed to optimistic, estimate of potential crowds should be made, then choose a site that will accommodate approximately twenty-five percent fewer people than the anticipated attendance. If you get a larger crowd, you can always fit it in. However, there's nothing worse than overestimating your crowd, and compounding the mistake by having it appear to be even smaller than your expectations because it's overwhelmed by the size of your site. If you should fall into this sad circumstance, there are ways to make the crowd appear to be larger than it is. Make every effort to reduce the size of the appearance of the hall. For instance: rather than having the podium on the stage, move the podium to the floor; keep the curtain closed if it's in a high school gymnasium with a stage; spread the chairs apart, both between rows and between chairs; leave the bleachers along the walls closed rather than open so that those who cannot sit will be forced to stand along the side making them feel more a part of the crowd; douse the lights over the balcony, or any unfilled sections of the hall, and attempt to have the brightest lights on those parts that are filled. These preparations are important both for those who are attending—it gives a sense of being involved in something that is successful rather than a failure; and it's important for the media—it gives the sense that more people responded than you'd expected.

In 1972, George Wallace frequently underestimated his crowds intentionally so that he would be forced to speak two or three times to crowds of 1500 each, rather than one crowd of 4500, thus leaving the clear impression that the response to his campaign was much greater than he had expected.

Be aware of traffic patterns leading to the place where the rally is to be held, so people don't have to drive through tremendously heavy traffic coming to a rally. Check to make sure the parking arrangements are adequate for the anticipated crowd size. Check very carefully the built-in speaker system or the available amplifier and microphone to insure that they function adequately. It is bizarre, but a nation that can send a man to the moon is incapable of constructing an amplification and speaker system which accurately projects a person's voice and tone. Prepare a backup speaker system (in smaller auditoriums or outdoor rallies this may be simply an electric megaphone). Check that the stage area is large enough for the anticipated number of speakers, and introducers. The number of people on stage should be kept as small as possible, commensurate with political needs. If you can keep it to six or eight, you make a much better appearance than if the stage is crowded with thirty or forty people. Check with the media for their requirements to insure that you can provide adequate lighting capacity and space for the press. Check out and clear any necessary permits for fund solicitation —it would be a shame to have a large sympathetic crowd together and not be permitted to take a collection. Check the history of the auditorium to be sure that you're not speaking in a segregated club or at a place where there is a union on strike.

In short, before choosing the site, insure that all possible contingencies are provided for and all arrangements are very, very carefully made.

Assuming that you have found a good site, you must then work to build a crowd two to three times the auditorium size, presupposing that actual attendance will be one-third to one-half of the projected attendance. If it rains, if you don't get as much press coverage for the rally as you think you should, if the local ball team is playing a home game, if streets in the area are suddenly closed for repairs, your crowd could fall apart. Always assume that the worst could happen, so build your crowd bigger than necessary. If they all show up, so much the better.

The most common way to build a crowd is to

leaflet the community. Leafleting is discussed fully in Chapter 5, however, factories, shopping areas, door-to-door drops, parking lots and generally any area where people congregate should all be covered. On the day of the rally leaflet very heavily close to the rally location at a time close to the hour of the rally.

Think creatively. Use five times as many leaflets as you think you should. Tack leaflets to telephone poles near bus stops and other places where people are likely to see them on the day of the rally. However, you must be prepared to clean up afterwards.

The second basic crowd builder is the telephone. Begin a telephone tree, calling one person, asking them to call five people, and asking each of those people to call two and so on. Start with your list of known supporters, then go to your list of potential supporters, and continue to lists of potentially sympathetic organizations in the area. Hopefully other organizations will be willing to call their supporters on your behalf. If not, acquire their lists and do it yourself, giving your supporters names to call.

Third, use posters—on bulletin boards in schools and factories, at businesses, in downtown store windows, in car windows, any place that a poster may be seen, put a poster.

Fourth, if local tradition and custom permit, and if you have checked to be sure that it is legal and you have all the necessary permits, use sound trucks. Go through neighborhoods near the site of the rally on the day preceding it and again shortly before the rally begins.

Fifth, use radio and newspaper ads judiciously. You may be able to get a great deal of free publicity out of the use of beeper phones and talk shows as a way of announcing your rally. However, it may be necessary to purchase ads.

Two general rules apply: for newspaper ads, the bolder the type, and the less type there is, the better received the ad is likely to be—it catches people's eyes, stops them as they go by, and gives the necessary information in one quick glance. This is vastly superior to attempting to make a well-reasoned argument in the ad which would convince people to come.

On the radio, do short spots; twenty or thirty seconds is best. If your radio station offers a package of times be wary of it. Instead use primarily driving times, seven to nine in the morning, four to six in the evening, and some mid-morning time for people who are home listening to their radios. Concentrate your effort in the last two or three days during those prime time slots, particularly drive time.

Sixth, issue group invitations, especially to schools and nursing homes. Explain to school principals that it may be the only chance that their students have to hear the next president or the next senator or the next congressman; and that it will be an opportunity for the students to express themselves on the critical issues of the day. A great many old people have very little to do with their days, and given an opportunity (including transportation if necessary) they will be willing to attend rallies. Have other organizations issue invitations on your behalf, such as PTA and church groups. Get their leaders committed to bringing their members to your rally.

Seventh, car caravans are sometimes useful in building crowds. If you can get enough cars headed toward a final wrapup rally the night before the election or another major event, you'll usually pick up cars along the way.

And finally, use stunts and imaginative gimmicks. Airplane banners, lights late at night (as movie theatres sometimes use), parades, bands, whatever you can dream up should be used to get people to your rally.

When people get there, of course you must be ready for them. The tone of the rally itself can be very important. Always provide music—rock music, folk music, polka music, nostalgia music—geared to what you think your potential crowd would like to hear. You're better off if you have fewer speakers and more music. At peace and environmental rallies the high point is almost invariably the audience singing along with a folk-singer, or joining in the joy of listening to a rock band.

A strong element of communion and self-reinforcement is important for any rally, since it is vital for all of us to believe we are part of a worthy effort.

If there is to be more than one or two speakers, they should be instructed to be as brief as possible, to keep their remarks on the topic, not to stray into a general discussion of the state of the world, and not to demagogue and harangue the people. This does not mean that the speakers have to be dull and boring. It is possible to be exciting while saying something substantive and non-demagogic.

Finally, prepare plenty of signs, posters, banners for the hall, decorations—anything to add to the mood. This specifically does not include the passing out of party hats and party favors. There's a fine line between creating the spirit of joy and movement, and cheap gimmickry. Here again, your discretion must be the final judge.

5

CANVASSING AND ELECTION DAY

"There's only one way to hold a district: you must study human nature and act accordin'. You can't study human nature in books. Books is a hindrance more than anything else. To learn real human nature you have to go among the people, see them and be seen. I know every man, woman, and child in the Fifteenth District, except them that's been born this summer—and I know some of them, too. I know what they like and what they don't like, what they are strong at and what they are weak in, and I reach them by approachin' at the right side."

GEORGE WASHINGTON PLUNKETT

In recent years the principles and processes of canvassing have developed a mystique of their own. The canvass is thought to be the all-powerful tool used by insurgents in breaking political organizations and electing their candidates. All the media, traditional, ethnic, patronage bound, bad-guy candidates are supposed to buckle under the power of magic canvass.

Two things have been forgotten in all the hoopla. First, the canvass has been the basic tool of political organization from time immemorial. It is no more than a systematic way of finding out where your supporters are and keeping track of them. Second, the canvass is worthless unless you get the votes out on election day. The election day operation has rarely been discussed, yet a canvass without an election day operation is nothing more than an opinion survey.

A canvass can be used only if you have a relatively long time to organize and/or a rather large body of volunteers. It is difficult to canvass effectively if you have only a few volunteers, because only canvassing results of the last ten days or two weeks before election day reflect the view of the voters on election day. It is not a crime to be unable to canvass and there are other ways to fill the void left by lack of a thorough canvass.

LEAFLETING

Levels of campaigning are determined in large part by the availability of money and energy, which are almost (but not quite) interchangeable in politics. The most basic level of involvement of workers and voters is that of literature distribution. Leafleting is critically important in a campaign in which few people know your candidate. You should think seriously about using a saturation leafleting schedule early, in the hopes of generating interest in your candidate. As you near election day people will ask more sophisticated questions than those which will be answered in the early leaflet, and it will be necessary to prepare a more substantive piece, but it is good to start with a relatively simple two-sided leaflet or three-panel pamphlet.

You should begin in those areas where you have the highest potential support. If you have a candidate who is a union member, for instance, you may want to start leafleting at factory gates. If you have a candidate who is primarily concerned about consumer issues, you may want to start at the shopping centers and supermarkets.

The literature which you use to leaflet will be determined, obviously, by your potential constituency. This is not because you are interested in hiding the candidate's record or views on any particular subject, but simply because it makes most sense to make information about the issues which concern them most available to people. To leaflet in a black area with literature about wilderness preservation simply doesn't speak to the issues which will be of foremost concern.

In addition to using leafleting for early awareness building, you may want to use it as a supplement regularly through the campaign. It gives volunteers a chance to get out and meet people; it keeps the level of awareness high; it supplements canvassing in those areas where you cannot reach everybody; and it gives an impression of energy and involvement in the community.

In distributing the leaflets, you first need to find the best places. Most Chambers of Commerce have a list of factories in the area with a hundred or more employees. Sometimes the list will even tell the number of employees and it will almost certainly give the telephone number of the plant and the plant manager. Call the plant, check shift times and the approximate number of people on each shift. Arrive early and check with entering workers or guards at the gates about which gates will have the largest flow of people at the shift change. If there are walk-in gates, start thirty minutes or so before the shift change and leaflet people on the way in. This way as workers change clothes or sit around shooting the breeze before work, they have something in hand to look at, to read, to talk to other people about before the work day starts.

Leafleting on the way out is a more difficult process. People tend to sprint away from their jobs, literally on the run for a bus, a car or a bar. Do not be surprised if they brush by rather brusquely.

Shopping centers are, in most cases, technically private property and the management can prohibit you from leafleting there if they wish to do so, and some do. The prohibition is almost always explained as a way of keeping litter off the streets. It is virtually never uniformly enforced against all candidates or political causes—simply those with which ownership or management disagrees. Local people will sometimes know which shopping centers will permit you to leaflet and which ones will not. If you don't know, simply call and ask. Some centers will have a "community booth" from which to work. However, reservations are usually required for these facilities.

Any large gathering of people—sporting events, concerts, theatres—provide an opportunity for you to contact a large number of people quickly. Sometimes these will be very sympathetic audiences. In

1972 the leafleting of lines outside of "A Clockwork Orange" turned out to be a very lucrative source of volunteers for McCarthy. I suspect the same would have been true for the McGovern campaign but not for the Nixon campaign. Think about the people who will be present in an area, think about their concerns, and then think about whether they are likely voters for your candidate before determining priorities for the use of manpower.

You may also want to leaflet with the candidate by preceding him or her on the street during a handshaking tour. In this way people are prepared for the shock of an outstretched hand and a smiling face saying, "Hi! I'm Candidate Plunkett." You will also want to use leafleting for specific events, which is discussed in the preceding chapter.

THE TELEPHONE CANVASS

The next level of organization is a telephone canvass, which makes it possible to canvass large areas with limited manpower and without asking people to leave their houses.

To do this, you need a reverse directory (directory of listings by addresses), sometimes available from the telephone company, or a city directory with telephone numbers copied into it from the phone book by volunteers. If you have a final voting list, you can simply put numbers on it and call from that. If registration is still open, or if it is still possible for people to change registration from one party to another, it is, however, necessary to use the reverse directory or city directory.

In addition to calling lists, some other information should be on hand for telephone canvassers.

They will need lists of polling places, the hours polls are open, telephone numbers for the registrar of voters, rules regarding absentee ballots, information about the candidate's stand on the most prominent issues and a current schedule of radio and TV spots, if you have them.

While everyone develops their own particular style of talking to people on the telephone, the door-to-door canvassing "openers" suggested later in this chapter may be helpful on the telephone as well. Remember that you are catching people cold with a discussion that they had not anticipated—so talk *slowly, painfully slowly*. Provide opportunities for people to respond to what you have suggested, and provide opportunities for yourself to bail out. One way to do that is to first introduce yourself, say why you are calling, ask them to consider your candidate, and then pause for a moment; if you get a negative response, thank them for their time and hang up. If you get no response or a non-committal response, you can continue by encouraging the person to attend an event, such as the opening of a storefront, or by inviting them to hear the candidate on radio or television spots or at an event in the local area. Then thank the person for their time and trouble. If you get a positive response, ask the person for help in phoning or in the office, and follow up on it. After completing the phone call, mark the voter list as outlined below and proceed from there as with a door-to-door canvass.

One common misuse of the telephone is the "blind" (or phony) early canvass. The voters are called two or three months early and told that you are from an opinion survey firm (fabricating the name of a supposedly professional firm) and then questioned about preferences, simply to determine the level of name recognition, or favorable or unfavorable response. My own feeling is that this kind of device should not be used, since it can frequently backfire if the press learns of it. You're better off just being flat out with people, telling them why you're calling, who you're calling for, and asking them whatever you want to know.

THE KENNEDY CANVASS

The next level of volunteer voter contact is the so-called Kennedy Canvass. The origins of the term and the concept are lost in antiquity (about twelve years ago). It requires more energy than leafleting, slightly more energy than telephone canvassing, and a high level of name recognition of your candidate since you need to recruit volunteers off the phone. However, if you have an ideological candidate who is likely to generate volunteers easily, it is possible to use a Kennedy Canvass successfully even if you do not have enough workers to do a full telephone canvass because as you call, you pick up additional workers.

To do the Kennedy Canvass, take a reverse directory, check against a map which shows blocks, and start calling around the block. Ask people their views, and as soon as you have a favorable response, ask if they would be willing to distribute literature to the other people on their block. As soon as you find one person to do that, send or deliver to them a prepared packet of materials including literature, duplicates of the voter lists for the block, buttons, bumperstickers, and any other materials that you might want distributed. From then on that person is your block worker. Hopefully, you will be able to follow up with them on a regular basis and they will turn out to be trustworthy, loyal, helpful, friendly, courteous, kind, cheerful, thrifty, brave, clean, and reverent. Of course, a large number of them turn out to be duds who never follow up on their own. Still you will have reached more people than you would have otherwise. Even though it's not as good as it should be, it's better than not getting to those people at all.

THE DOOR-TO-DOOR CANVASS

The last and most effective level is the door-to-door canvass. If, after discussing it, thinking about it, working on it, getting *all* your people together and talking and working out the energy requirement, you think you have enough manpower for this, proceed as follows:

More often than not your volunteers will be canvassing precincts or blocks other than their own. You may be, however, in the fortuitous circumstance of being able to cover each precinct with local people. Assume that you will not be that lucky and that you will have to use people who do not live in the neighborhood, are probably not familiar with the area, and usually have never done canvassing work before.

First, you need to assemble the following materials:

1. Maps of the areas on a block by block basis. These are frequently available from a city planning department in large or medium size cities, from the state highway department, from gas stations, or from the Chamber of Commerce. Attempt to obtain as many free copies as you can. However if they cost money, get one good copy and have copies made.

2. Voters lists, normally available from the registrar of voters, are ordered by street address. You will need lists of both parties if you are in a

primary in which cross-over voting is permitted or if it is a general election.

3. Manila file folders, pencils, an adequate supply of literature for each house which you anticipate canvassing, and some buttons and bumperstickers for canvassers to give to supporters, as well as "not-at-home" cards.

4. "Issue sheets" so that your canvassers will know something about what the candidate is saying, together with printed copies of canvassing instructions.

Once your materials are together, select priority areas so that in case you do not finish your canvassing, you will have at least started in the areas which are potentially most vote-rich for your candidate. You can select those areas on the basis of past elections where similar candidates have done well, by votes on issues (such as referendums) where your candidate has a clear position and the opponent has an opposing position; or those areas where the party vote in the general election was strongest.

For each area to be canvassed you will need to prepare what is called (for reasons which are now obscure) a "hard card." A hard card is in reality a manila file folder. On the left hand inside of the file folder staple a map marked to show the precise area to be covered. On the right hand inside attach the voter registration list (duplicated on the same magic copier) cut so that approximately fifty households, or fifty to seventy voters, are included on each hard card. This is approximately the number of houses which can be covered in one day in an area of mixed single-family and multiple-family dwellings in a moderately urbanized area. In an urban area which consists of large apartment houses you can include more names, and in a wealthier or rural area where the houses are more scattered, put fewer names on the hard card.

Each hard card should include voters from only one precinct. Don't cross precinct lines in a canvasser's assignment.

In addition, write on the manila folder or a mimeographed sheet stapled inside the folder the location of the polling place for that precinct, and the polling hours; a brief summary of local registration laws (i.e., how many days a person must live in the state, county, and precinct in order to vote); and the location and hours of the nearest place where they can register to vote. Also put in each manila folder a few fliers, bumperstickers, and buttons. If you have a schedule of TV and radio advertisements in advance, include it with each hard card. If the candidate is scheduled to appear in the area, give that information to the canvassers so they can encourage people to participate in the up-coming event. *Be sure* to have the phone number and address of your headquarters on each hard card.

Mark on the outside flap of the hard card the precinct and, if it is broken down lower than a precinct level, the specific streets and addresses of that hard card so you can file it easily.

Once you have collected these materials and prepared the hard card, you are ready to begin briefing the canvassers. It may be helpful to mimeograph briefing instructions to avoid the necessity of repeating them endlessly. However, if you mimeograph them, insist that the canvassers read them before leaving on their rounds so that if any thing is unclear, questions can be asked rather than blundering and operating in the blind. Obviously, in the final analysis, you have to trust the good judgment of the canvasser since not everything can be covered, but they should be as well prepared as possible.

Canvassers should be instructed to go to each house (even those not on their voters' list) if registration is still open or if the list is not the most recent or final one.

Once at a house, the canvasser should look for its daily entrance. It may not be the front door, but rather the side door next to the driveway. If the canvasser can be helpful, of course, he or she should be. If you arrive as the lady or man of the house is arriving with the groceries, it doesn't cost anything to help carry them. Be polite, help in whatever little way is possible, even by picking up the newspaper and giving it to them at the door.

Canvassers should avoid talking to landlords in large apartment buildings since almost invariably the landlords will tell them that they can't come in. Just go in if the main entrance to the building is open. If the building has a buzzer system, you might try pushing one of the buttons (particularly one with names of two different people who are obviously roommates rather than relatives) and tell them why you're there. Frequently, in the first three or four tries, somebody will push the button to let you in the main entrance. Be explicit and professional when you identify yourself. Mention the name and location of your organization to help assure the resident that you are here for a legitimate purpose.

Once you arrive at the voter's door, you should again introduce yourself by name, saying that you are a volunteer for Plunkett, who is seeking the office of president in the election on November 7th, 1972, or whenever. Check to be sure that the person you are talking to is the person listed on your hard card. Suggest that you would like to discuss the candidate's views on the issues in the campaign. This is a rather sensitive point because historically canvassers have been urged to be non-ideological interviewers. There are two things wrong with that. First, it is ideological people of both the right and the left who actually do the work of the parties, and do it for ideological reasons, and it is the most ideologically attuned voters who vote. It is wrong to pretend otherwise. Second, a campaign should be about more than simply a candidate—it should try to raise issues of substance. As a consequence, it is my feeling and experience that you should not hesitate to talk about issues.

You should not be argumentative, or "hard" in such a way as to drive people inevitably and invariably away from your campaign, but you should say that you want to talk about issues and then ask for a few minutes of their time. If you pause at that point most people will respond, either by inviting you in or telling you to get lost. If they respond negatively—"they're busy," "they don't want to vote," "they never vote," "they're apathetic," "they don't care," or that "they're going to vote for your opponent"—think of a second opening if you can. If the response is still negative, thank them for their time, give them some literature, say you hope they'll consider your candidate and look at the issues involved—and leave. If, on the other hand, they are receptive— "they don't know but they'd like to know," "they plan to vote but haven't decided for whom"—and then invite you in, by all means go in. Take a few minutes of your time and theirs to talk about the campaign. This does not mean that you should engage in a marathon discussion session. We live in a sad time in which many people find themselves very lonely, and given the opportunity will bend your ear for the remainder of the day. If you want to return to talk to them out of a measure of human kindness, that's good, but in the process of canvassing (unless you plan to return on a regular basis to that same neighborhood) you shouldn't spend your time just talking.

You obviously should not attempt to sell people politics in the way they would be sold a new car. Be soft and understated in what you say. Attempt to let them talk and feel out their opinion. Explain to them that you think that their vote is very important and that you're concerned about how they vote. Hope that by their response you will be able to determine how they will finally vote.

It is neither necessary nor advisable to ask people directly how they will vote.

Occasionally they will offer their opinion in a positive way and say that they are really concerned about the candidate and what he or she represents. At that point you can escalate a bit by asking if they would be willing to help the campaign in some way. Start with the easiest things and work your way up. Ask them to make some phone calls from their house. If they say yes, ask them if they would be willing to have a coffee klatsch in their home, and then ask them to put it together as well as host it. Volunteer to help in its organization. Work up to the possibility of their taking precinct responsibility or an even more major responsibility in the campaign as they prove themselves. If given an opportunity to involve themselves in the campaign, people often will take it.

Avoid state and local issues if you're not familiar with them. If you're from outside of the area or haven't been following things closely, don't get into long discussions or provide arguments. You should know the candidate's views on a number of issues and be prepared to discuss them with the voter, but once again, do not be argumentative in the way you present them. Feel free to make your views clear, but in such a way as to insure that he will go out and vote for your opponent. Be sure to thank the voter for his time when the conversation is through. Assure them that rides and babysitters will be available on election day and that you will be back in contact with them to see if they need either of those services.

Occasionally a voter will offer contributions for the campaign to the canvasser, and there are two schools of thought on how to handle this. One holds that the canvasser should never accept a contribution from the voter. I do not belong to that school, but feel instead that you have entrusted the canvasser with probably the sole visual and personal representation of the campaign to the voter, and if you have entrusted him or her with a person's vote, there is no reason not to entrust him or her with a few dimes or dollars of that voter's money if the voter wants to contribute it. That money should be returned to headquarters, reported, and a "thank you" note sent at once.

If the voter is not home, leave a pre-printed notice like the kind the telephone company leaves —a sheet of paper with a round hole and slash at the top to put on the door handle. On one side leave the message that you were there, no one was home, and you'll be back in touch with them. On the other side you may include information about your candidate and the phone number and address of your headquarters.

Once the canvasser leaves, he or she should complete the hard card. The voter should be put into one of four categories: 1, marked on the hard card is definitely a vote for your candidate; 2, probably a vote for your candidate; 3, unable to determine the voter's preference (they are apathetic or genuinely undecided); 4, definitely opposed to your candidate or supporting the opponent. In addition, in those cases where you did not talk to the voters you need a couple of other marks: *N/A* if there is no answer, you couldn't find the house, there's no one home, and so on; *M* for moved, which will give you the basis for challenge of the voter lists if that person in fact votes on election day, since we are presuming that you would not be so unscrupulous as to send someone to vote in the place of a person who has moved; and *D*, deceased, marked for the same reason as you marked the *M* and on the same presumption. If you can't decide which category to put the voter in use the following: if the choice is between a *1* and a *2*, use *2*; if between a *2* and a *3*, use *3*; if between a *3* and a *4*, use a *3*. This is because in many cases, the *2s* and *3s* will be contacted again in a continuing effort to persuade them, and the *1s* will be contacted and asked to help work in one way or another.

After returning to headquarters at the end of the day, the canvasser should immediately follow up on special requests of that day. If a voter needed information on a particular issue, it should be mailed out right then; if a voter volunteered to help with something, that should be noted immediately, put into the volunteer file, and the person called within forty-eight hours. All follow-ups should be done immediately, or they'll never get done.

Once that is done, the canvasser should be debriefed. Discuss with him or her what kinds of issues concerned the voters he spoke with, what kind of response the candidate's name got, what kinds of information people sought, and the general tone of the neighborhood. Only in that way can you get a more comprehensive picture of what voters are thinking than can be gathered by the sort of random sample taken sitting in cabs, buses, and bars. In addition, you may be able to help a canvasser who is discouraged by letting him see where other people have been successful and learning from them what kinds of approaches and issues have interested the voters they've spoken to.

In 1964, during the campaign in California on a fair housing referendum, a number of canvassers had been very successful in talking to people but one in particular had come back with negative results and was very discouraged. We asked what approach he had used at the voters' doors. He said that his opening line was, "Hi! I'm here to talk to you about Proposition 14 which is an effort by the racists in the state to take away everything that's been gained in the last hundred years." As you might imagine, that was not a line which opened a lot of doors.

Once the canvass, immediate follow-up, and debriefing have been completed and the hard card returned to its file, you can begin planning the follow-up to the door-to-door canvass. Start by calling all of the N/A's using the basic telephone canvass outlined earlier. Mark the response as though the person had responded in the door-to-door canvass. If you have enough volunteers to continue the canvass by foot, of course you will want to try again to reach the N/As at their door, with the added advantage that the first canvasser will have left a note and literature. Once this second canvassing round is completed, hard cards should be refiled in a section for complete cards in anticipation of election day.

THE PRE-ELECTION DAY CANVASS

On the Sunday before the election, start in the early afternoon to telephone your definite yeses (1s). This process will continue for forty-eight hours until approximately noon of election day. The purpose of this phone call is to remind people to vote and do a survey of babysitting and transportation needs for election day.

The important things to cover in that conversation are a simple introduction of yourself by name as a volunteer for Plunkett, a reminder to the voter to vote on election day, and an offer of a ride to the polls or a babysitter for the day. Don't specifically ask the person to vote for your candidate. Presumably they're committed to him or you wouldn't be calling. If a person needs a babysitter or transportation on election day make a note of it, confirm the person's address and the time of day that the service will be needed. Immediately transfer that information to a master sheet in the office showing the total need for rides and babysitting on election day. Be prepared to provide information on polling places, absentee ballots, and other election day details. It is virtually impossible to be too polite or to talk too slowly over the telephone and in the haste of the last moment that must be remembered. Once the entire hard card is completed you file it in yet another place identified as "Canvassing Forms, Phoning Completed." After this round of phoning the canvassing is completed, and you are ready for the election day "pulling" to begin.

ELECTION DAY

Preparations for election day should begin well ahead of time. While it is virtually impossible to have a good election day operation without first having a good canvass operation, the election operation alone can produce as much as five to ten percent additional vote for your candidate. Detailed preparation well in advance is essential to the success of the operation.

Recruiting volunteers for election day should begin early, and specific assignments made as soon as possible. For each polling place you will need, at the minimum, the following: one precinct house (a house in that precinct as near as possible to the polling place which can be used throughout the period of time that the polls are open); one leafleter; one pollwatcher, who must in most instances be a registered voter; one driver with a car; a coordinator of the election day operation for that precinct; and a couple of pullers. You can use more than this if it is possible to get them. If the polls are open for twelve hours it is preferable to allow people, particularly those who are pollwatching and leafleting, to work in shifts. You will need a few people, usually not more than three or four, at central headquarters on election day simply to answer telephone calls from people who have requests for information about voting places; to answer questions from precinct captains; and to provide a central legal source on election law.

You need to begin early the legal preparations

for election day. In some states the secretary of state's available summary of election law will be quite adequate, but you should check it against the law itself.

If any changes are needed, make them and then prepare a summary for use in each precinct house. Have a complete text of the law available at the central headquarters on election day, and if possible have a competent lawyer on hand. These preparations are especially important in an area where there is a tradition of election fraud or simply one of inefficiency and breakdowns. Occasionally the law can protect from simple ineptitude as well as from fraud. Hubert Humphrey in the 1972 Ohio primary, for instance, was able to force the reopening of many polls because machines were delivered with votes already on them, locked, unlockable, or otherwise inoperative.

By election day, the precinct houses should have the lists of the *1* and *2* voters and their phone numbers for that precinct. Any special needs that have been determined, such as rides or baby-sitters, should be indicated, including the time the services are needed. Where you do not have precinct houses, it will be necessary to run the election day operations from the central headquarters. You may be able to get along with fewer people this way simply because you can use your resources more efficiently, keep the drivers driving more consistently, and generally maintain a smooth flow of services.

On election day two people per precinct will be necessary early in the morning,—a leafleter and a poll-watcher. The leafleter should be carefully instructed to obey all relevant state election day laws about distances from the polling place, instructing voters in the use of the voting machine and state laws concerning campaign materials in the voting booth. The leafleter should have a sample ballot or palm card to give voters. This sample ballot should show the name of your candidate and how to either mark it on the ballot or pull the lever on the voting machine to vote for him or her. (The best way to do this is to print it as the ballot for that polling place is printed—this information is available from the Registrant of Voters—only gray-out the other names and print your candidate's name in a bolder type face.) Palm cards occasionally have a picture of the candidate and a slogan as well as the sample ballot.

Legal provisions for pollwatchers vary from one state to the next, but Mary Meehan accurately summarized the general rules in this way in her manual for the New Democratic Coalition: "The poll-watcher must be certified by the election board or a court clerk. He is allowed to be at the polling place before the polls open and to check the voting machines or ballot boxes. For example, he checks the machine counters to make sure they are on zero; he looks inside the booth to make certain all levers are working properly. While the polls are open he is normally allowed to stand or sit in the polling room near the election officials, but he must not speak with any voters, campaign in any way, or block the path of the voters as they go to the booth. A poll watcher does not always have the right to challenge voters, but usually does have the right to seek arrest if the violation is blatant. He generally has the right to check the totals on the machines or to watch the counting of the paper ballots after the polls close." *

*CANVASSING AND ELECTION DAY by Mary Meehan; Copyright 1970 by the New Democratic Coalition, St. Louis, Mo.; mimeographed.

136

Approximately four or five hours before the polls close the list of people who have voted is picked up by a runner from the precinct house. The runner returns the list to the precinct house, and from the house the precinct is pulled. As in pre-election canvassing, there are two ways to do pulling: by foot and by phone. With the first, a person is sent to the door of the 1 and 2 voters who have not yet voted to remind them to do so. For the people not at home, the pullers take with them a card (similar to a canvassing door card) slit at the top so that it can be put on the door knob. The message on the card is that a campaign volunteer from the Plunkett for President campaign was there to encourage them to vote (if they have not yet done so) with information on what hours the polls are open, the location of their polling place, and the telephone number of your precinct house in case they need a ride or a baby-sitter or other services.

The second kind of puller is a phone puller. If you do not have enough people to pull by foot or if it's too late in the day to get to all of the houses, you can call each voter, tell them whom you are calling for, remind them to vote, and offer them services. In some cases a bit of persistence may be necessary, although it obviously must be polite since you want the voters to vote for your candidate when they get to the polling places. Frequently it will be necessary to encourage them to vote and to explain to them the importance of their single vote, and how much your candidate is relying on it.

The tasks of babysitters and drivers are clear. If you give the central headquarters number for those who want a ride or a babysitter, the central headquarters will then call into the precinct house to assign drivers or a babysitter. Alternatively, you may wish to leave your precinct house telephone number with the voters during canvassing. It is not uncommon to advertise the telephone numbers to be called on election day for babysitters and drivers. Very few voters will call for these services if they do not intend to vote for your candidate. However, it is important to check local customs and law because some places prohibit the provision of these services, others prohibit advertising the availability of them. The most efficient use of a driver is simply to have them wait outside while the voter votes, unless the lines are very long and they can use their time more efficiently to pick up another voter.

Remember margins of five to ten percent are very common and if these election day tasks are done well, it can make the difference between a marginal defeat and a substantial victory.

At the end of the day the poll watcher remains at the polling place while the votes are either read off the machine, or the paper ballots are counted by hand. The poll watcher should remain at the polling place until that vote total has been called to the central election office. He or she should also call that vote total to your candidate's headquarters so you will have those totals available to check against the figures given by the central election office.

If you have done all of your other jobs well up to that point and have had a good candidate, a substantail streak of good luck, a little bit of money and the gods with you, you will be ready for an election eve party. It should be done well, for if it is, and you win in a primary campaign, it helps to generate morale for the on-going campaign. Assign that task to someone in the office who is more interested in doing that than anything else, but be sure that it's someone with imagination, good taste, and who is trustworthy. Frequently election eve parties are held at a local club or hotel and in all cases it is necessary for the candidate to make a short statement of concession (hold out as long as possible) or victory.

You may then go to sleep until the next morning when you must either begin campaigning again (if it was a primary) or begin the process of governing.

READER'S RESPONSE

To: Sam W. Brown, Jr.
    c/o PYRAMID COMMUNICATIONS, INC.
    919 Third Avenue
    New York, New York 10022

From: _____

      _____

      _____

      _____

Dear Sam:

☐ I tried the following idea and it worked like a charm. Why don't you include it in your manual when and if it is revised and up-dated.

☐ I tried the following idea from your manual and it didn't work at all. Scrap it!

☐ I tried the following idea from your manual and it worked pretty well, but we also improved on it. The improvement below should be included in the manual when and if it is revised and up-dated.

☐ Thought you might be interested in the following.

☐ I don't even like forms which attempt to be helpful.

I am starting on another sheet.

_____

_____

_____

_____

_____

_____

_____

_____

_____

_____

_____

_____

Peace,

_____

Date: _____